Green Line 3

Green Line 4

1 Famous athletes: A quiz

a) *Look at these athletes and match them with the right text. Write the correct number in the box.*

1. Usain Bolt 2. Roger Federer 3. Lionel Messi 4. Serena Williams
5. Dirk Nowitzki 6. Michael Phelps 7. Lindsey Vonn 8. Sebastian Vettel

She's an American ski racer and has won 50 world cup races in her career. ☐	He's an American swimmer and has won more than 15 Olympic gold medals. ☐	He plays for FC Barcelona and is captain of the Argentina national team. ☐	He plays for the Dallas Mavericks and he's 2.13 m tall. ☐
He's from Jamaica and holds the world record in the 100- and 200-metre sprints. ☐	She has won more than 26 Grand Slam titles and is a tennis player from America. ☐	He's a tennis player and in 2008 he won 32 matches and didn't lose one! ☐	He's a German Formula 1 racing driver and was world champion in 2010 and 2011. ☐

b) *Now make sentences with relative clauses. Write them in your exercise book.*

Usain Bolt is the sprinter from Jamaica who holds the world record in the 100- and 200-metre sprints.

2 Tandem activity: A sports crossword puzzle

With a partner, take turns to explain your crossword puzzles to each other. Use relative clauses.

Example: It's a thing which you use … / It's a game which you can play with 11 people. / It's a person who can run …

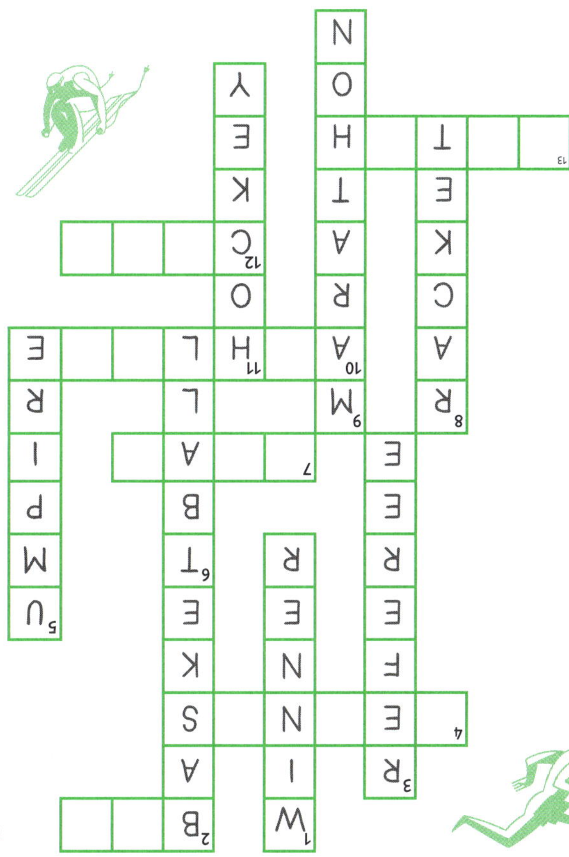

Green Line 3/4
Vertretungsstunden
ISBN: 978-3-12-560036-2

1 Working as a football reporter

a) *Read the speech bubbles. Who plays, who shoots the goals and who wins the match?*

b) *Put the speech bubbles in the right order. Write the numbers in the boxes.*

c) *What do the marked words mean? Explain them in English to your partner.*

d) *How would the reporter present the football commentary? Practise reading and try to make it as interesting as possible for the audience.*

Good evening. This is Peter Johnson, your **commentator**. Welcome to this match between Manchester United and Arsenal London, here at Etihad **Stadium** in Manchester.

Oh no, what's that? Miller is attacked by Brook. Foul! What is the referee going to do? He has seen it and blows his **whistle**. Yellow card for Brook and **penalty shot** for Arsenal.

The game starts. ManU's captain Manning **kicks off**.

Miller himself is going to do the penalty shot. ManU sets up a wall. Miller kicks the ball and it's a wonderful shot. O'Neil gets the ball; he's right in front of ManU's goal and scores. GOOOAAAL! It's the 63rd minute and that was the second goal of the match. A great goal by Tim O'Neil.

McAllister scores and … goal! Gooooaaal!!!! Goal for Manchester. A beautiful goal by Rob McAllister in the 25th minute.

Forty-two minutes gone. The score is still one-nil but Arsenal has got the ball. Miller passes the ball to O'Neil, but O'Neil **misses** the ball. And now there's ManU's **defender** Brook who wins back the ball.

Welcome back for the second **half** of the match here at Etihad Stadium in Manchester. The score is one-nil and ManU was the better team in the first half of the game.

Arsenal seems to be stronger in this second half of the match. Sixty-two minutes gone. Arsenal's **midfielder** Podaya passes to Miller. Miller is now with the ball in front of ManU's goal. But here comes Brook …

And that's the referee's whistle. The game is over. One-one at the end of a beautiful match here at Etihad Stadium in Manchester.

2 Germany plays England: Write your own football report

a) *Have a look at the pictures and write your own football report.*

1.

2.

3.

4.

b) *How does the game end? Finish the football commentary.*

ISBN: 978-3-12-560036-2

Looking at … Football

A When did people start to play football? It's difficult to answer that question. There are a lot of old games in which people kicked some kind of ball. The old Greeks and Romans played a kind of football, but they were allowed to use their hands. So it was more like an early version of rugby! Similar games were played all over the world: in Australia, in New Zealand, but also in China and Japan.

B In the Middle Ages[1] football was already popular in England. Young men from two different villages often played against each other. There were two teams who had to get the ball into the goal of the other team. But the game was different from today: Each village had as many players as they wanted, there was no pitch, the play could last many hours, and there were no real rules. Often the whole match ended in a fight with broken noses! The king and the church didn't like this game and so they didn't allow people to play it. But a lot of young men still played the game.

C In the 18th and 19th century[2] football was very popular at English public schools. Again there were two teams, a ball, and two sticks in the ground were the goal. Many teachers weren't happy about the game because so many players got hurt. In 1828 a new headmaster[3], Thomas Arnold, came to the public school of Rugby. He thought sport was very important for the boys and football a good way to teach the boys how to play in a team. When the boys left school and went to university[4] they had a problem: The boys from other schools also played football but they had different rules. In 1848 students at Cambridge University wrote down the first football rules: Now there were goals, two teams with 15 to 20 players, shirts in different colours for the different teams, and only the goalkeeper[5] was allowed to use his hands with the ball.

D Football became more and more popular. The first football club was the FC Sheffield in the North of England in 1857. It is still there today. In 1862 players of different football clubs met in London and founded[6] the FA, the Football Association, and made new rules. Football wasn't popular only with English boys; boys in other parts of Europe started to play it, too. In 1874 the teacher Konrad Koch brought a football from England to his new school in Braunschweig and taught the boys how to play. They liked it, but not everyone in Germany was happy about that: Many felt that the boys should do athletics and not run after a ball!

E Today, people not only in Germany and England but almost everywhere in the world are crazy about football. In Germany more than 6 million people play football in 27,000 football clubs. Many are big fans and watch every game on TV or even go and watch their team play live. The players in the big football clubs make a lot of money. Football isn't just a game anymore – it has become a big business[7]!

[1] **Middle Ages** ['mɪdl‿eɪdʒɪz] = Mittelalter • [2] **century** ['sentʃri] = Jahrhundert • [3] **headmaster** ['hedmɑːstə] = Schulleiter/-in • [4] **university** [ˌjuːnɪ'vɜːsətɪ] = Universität • [5] **goalkeeper** ['gəʊlkiːpə] = Torwart • [6] **to found** [faʊnd] = gründen • [7] **business** ['bɪznɪs] = Geschäft

a) *Read the text and match the headlines with the paragraphs. Put the letters A–E into the boxes.*

- Early ball games ☐
- Football at public schools ☐
- Football today ☐
- Football fights in the Middle Ages ☐
- Europe follows England's example ☐

b) *Summarize in one or two sentences what happened at different times in the history of football: BC (before Christ), in the Middle Ages, 18th and 19th century, in 1848, in 1857, in 1874, today.*

c) *Imagine you are a boy at an English public school in England in the 19th century. You write a letter to your friend back home and tell him about this new game – football – and how it is played.*

Start like this: Dear Thomas, I'm now at Eaton College in … At school we study hard but in our free time we often play a new game. It's called football and it's really fun. For football you need … *Go on.*

Green Line 3/4
Vertretungsstunden
ISBN: 978-3-12-560036-2

A trip to a museum

a) *Class 9a went to the museum. Look at the speech bubbles and write down what they were and weren't allowed to do; what they had to do; and what they were and weren't able to do. Use your exercise book.*

b) *What do you know about Roman children?*
What were they able to do that you can't? What did they have to do that you don't have to do?

c) *Kyle didn't go with the other children to the museum. Complete the gaps with the simple past or the past perfect and find out why not.*

Kyle wanted to leave the house when his mum saw that he ____________________ (not; clean) his shoes. He was late but he ____________________ (must) clean his shoes before he left the house. When Kyle ____________________ (arrive) at the bus stop his shoes were clean, but the bus ____________________ (already; go). He ____________________ (run) to school, but when he ____________________ (get) there his class ____________________ (already; leave) on the school bus. He had to stay at school. When it ____________________ (be) time to go home, Kyle ____________________ (not; learn) very much about the Romans, but his shoes were still clean.

d) *Look at the picture of Class 9a. Here they are on their way home from the museum. Look at their faces/ actions. What do you think had happened earlier at the museum? Write a short text. Be creative!*

Green Line 3/4
Vertretungsstunden
ISBN: 978-3-12-560036-2

Looking at … A famous person in history

Read these texts and answer the questions below.

The lady with the lamp

"Oh, I love James. He's so funny and kind. I want to marry him! I hope he asks me," said Frances.
"Why don't you ask him?" asked Florence, smiling.
"Oh, don't be silly. I can't ask a man to marry me. Women aren't allowed to do that. Women have to look nice, play the piano and paint! And a lady has to wait for a man to marry her. Oh, I wish I was a man. Or I wish I was beautiful like you and then I could choose anybody I wanted."
"Well, I'm not going to marry a man. I'm going to become a nurse and work in a hospital," replied Florence.
Frances laughed at first – women don't work – but then saw that Florence wasn't smiling.

Dear Frances,
It's quarter past one in the morning and I can't sleep. Klara has just died and I feel so sad, I just want to cry. She had six children and the youngest is only two weeks old. How will they survive without their mother? I want to look after them but I can't. Sometimes I'd just like to go home and forget all this. It's too much. It's too hard. Why does God[1] do this to people? But then I talk to Theodor Fliedner and I can see how we can improve things. He's such a good teacher and he's so kind and gentle. We have to teach people how to stay clean; to wash their hands when they have touched somebody who is ill; and to drink clean water. When I qualify as a nurse, I will leave Germany and go back to London and look after people there.
Is Mum still angry with me? I didn't want to hurt her, but I just had to come here and learn to become a nurse. God wanted it this way …

Dear Jenny,
Things have improved here. Some nurses have arrived and they can now look after us better so that not as many soldiers die every day. Florence Nightingale comes around every night with a lamp and looks after us. She gives us something to drink and talks to us. The pain is never as bad when she's there. My dearest Jenny, I, too, will survive but I have to prepare you for a shock. I now only have one leg. But the important thing is that I still love you. I know that life will not be so easy now. It will be more difficult to work and to live. If you never want to see me again, I will understand.
Your ever-loving Henry

[1] **God** [gɒd] = Gott

a) *Are these sentences true or false?*

	true	false
1. This story possibly happened in the last fifty years.		✔
2. Florence wanted to get married quickly.		
3. Florence believed in God.		
4. Florence learnt how to become a nurse in London.		
5. Florence Nightingale was 'the lady with the lamp'.		
6. Henry lost both his legs in the war.		

b) *What do these words mean in the text? Tick the right answers.*

1. lamp (line 39)	☐ Tablette	☐ Licht	☐ Messer
2. nurse (line 11)	☐ Pfarrerin	☐ Lehrerin	☐ Krankenschwester
3. qualify (line 29)	☐ berechtigt werden	☐ lernen	☐ unterrichten

c) *Write a short description of Florence Nightingale's life. What do you know about her?*
Think about:
- her family
- the places she went to
- her life
- her character

d) *Write a short description of the other characters: Frances, Theodor and Henry. What do you think they are like? What happens to them? Who else do they know?*

Green Line 3/4
Vertretungsstunden
ISBN: 978-3-12-560036-2

Tandem activity: Stratford-upon-Avon

Partner A

You have information about two places that you can visit in Stratford. Answer your partner's questions about them. Your partner has information about two ***other*** *places in Stratford. Ask your partner about them and complete the information.*

Boating on the Avon
The Avon is a beautiful river which goes through the centre of Stratford and past the biggest theatre in town. You can go on boats here from spring to autumn and row up and down the river. There's no better way to see Stratford.
Prices: 1 rowing boat: £ 7.50 per hour

Royal Shakespeare Company Theatre
There are three theatres in this building, so you can be sure you'll find something that you like. You'll be able to choose between Shakespeare's plays and more modern ones. You can also do courses at the theatre, or go on a tour there. The theatre is in the centre of town, near the river.
Tickets: from £ 20 Children: £ 12.50

Shakespeare's Birthplace

What can you do / see there? ____________________

____

How much does it cost? ____________________

____

Where is it? ____________________

Anne Hathaway's Cottage

What can you do / see there? ____________________

____

How much does it cost? ____________________

____

Where is it? ____________________

- -

Partner B

You have information about two places that you can visit in Stratford. Answer your partner's questions about them. Your partner has information about two ***other*** *places in Stratford. Ask your partner about them and complete the information.*

Shakespeare's Birthplace
William Shakespeare was born in this house in 1564. This is also where he lived with his wife Anne Hathaway for the first five years. You can go on tours of the house and find out about his life and how he lived here. It is in the centre of town.
Prices:
Adults: £ 12.50 Children: £ 7.50
Shakespeare Pass (3 Shakespeare houses in a day):
Adults: £ 19 Children: £ 10

Anne Hathaway's Cottage
This is the place where Shakespeare's wife lived before she married him. It is a mile away from Stratford. You can look around the house and feel what life was like at the time. In the beautiful garden you can find out more about Shakespeare's plays.
Prices: Adults: £ 7.50
Children: £ 4.50

Boating on the Avon

What can you do / see there? ____________________

____

How much does it cost? ____________________

Where is it? ____________________

Royal Shakespeare Company Theatre

What can you do / see there? ____________________

____

How much does it cost? ____________________

Where is it? ____________________

Green Line 3/4
Vertretungsstunden
ISBN: 978-3-12-560036-2

1 All about Michelle

a) *Complete the gaps with the correct reflexive pronoun, 'each other' nothing (–).*

Michelle is now six years old and she has changed ________________ a lot. She can look after ________________. She's very clean and she washes ________________ a lot. She can feed ________________, too, but mum usually feeds her. My brother is nine years old and he and Michelle often play with ________________. They usually enjoy ________________ but my brother isn't always nice to her. Michelle can even go out alone. She and her friends often meet ________________ in our garden but sometimes they fight and hurt ________________. Then my mum runs out and shouts, "Can't you behave ________________?" Michelle never gets ________________ lost, and when she comes in, she sits ________________ down on the sofa and relaxes ________________. We all love Michelle and although she's just a cat, she's still part of the family.

b) *Write down everything you did today in German. Then write it in English. Underline all the reflexive verbs in the German and in the English texts.*

Meine Mutter hat mich um 6:30 geweckt und dann ... ________________

2 The Patterson family

a) *Read the play "Home alone" again and complete the sentences.*

1. If Grandpa was able to look after himself, he ________________ his home.
2. If the cleaning lady hadn't told Terry and Sally about Grandpa's problem, they ________________ ________________ him.
3. Mel and Amy won't be able to have their own rooms if Grandpa ________________ ________________.
4. They would probably have had more fun at the party if their parents ________________ ________________ again.

b) *Partner work! Write some questions for your partner. Start like this:*

What would you have done if ...?
What will you do if ...?
What would you do if ...?

c) *Now answer your partner's questions.*

ISBN: 978-3-12-560036-2

An argument

Read the story and answer the questions.

"Look at him. Isn't he good-looking?" Jeanie asked.

"Yes, he is," said Ella, "but I don't think he likes me."

Jeanie was showing Ella photos of her and her new boyfriend. Ella felt a bit jealous, of course. Jeanie often went out with Harvey now, and not with her.

"He likes you, but he's a bit jealous," Jeanie answered, "because you're my best friend."

"If I had a boyfriend, we could all go out together," said Ella. "Saturdays are usually a bit boring now. Nobody wants to go out with me."

"I know. Let's go out this Saturday. I'm going for a hike with my parents in the afternoon, but I'll call you when I get back. We could go to the cinema," suggested Jeanie.

On Saturday evening Ella waited for Jeanie to call. She waited and waited but Jeanie didn't call. Ella got angrier and angrier. "What kind of friend is that? She's probably gone out with Harvey and forgotten me," she thought. When the phone rang, she was so angry that she almost didn't answer it. When she answered it, it wasn't Jeanie, it was Jack.

"Do you want to come to the cinema with me?" asked Jack. "I've got two tickets but my friend Henry's ill and can't come."

Two hours later Ella and Jack went to the cinema together. They also saw Jeanie and Harvey there.

At school on Monday Ella heard Jeanie tell a friend that she'd had a great day on Saturday.

"I'm glad that you had a good day, Jeanie. I'm sure it would have been boring if you'd gone out with me."

"What's your problem? First you tell me that I never go out with you and then you can't even wait for me to call you!" replied Jeanie. "When I called you, your parents said that you'd already gone out."

"I waited until 6 pm but you didn't call. I knew you *really* wanted to go out with Harvey. Boyfriends are more important than best friends, of course," said Ella angrily.

"Oh, you always talk badly about Harvey. Just because *you* haven't got a boyfriend! Or you *didn't* have a boyfriend. But as soon as a boy asks you, you forget about me, don't you?" shouted Jeanie.

"Oh, that's just so unfair! And I thought you were my best friend. Well, not now!" shouted Ella back and walked away.

a) *Answer the questions below with words or phrases.*

1. How did Ella feel about Harvey? ____________________
2. What did Jeanie do on Saturday? ____________________
3. Why did Ella feel angry on Saturday? ____________________
4. Who did Ella go to the cinema with? ____________________
5. Why didn't Jack go with Henry? ____________________
6. Did Jeanie call Ella? ____________________

✎ b) *What did Jeanie and Ella do wrong when they were fighting on Monday?*

Jeanie	Ella
____________________	____________________
____________________	____________________
____________________	____________________

✎ c) *Write the conversation again. This time, the girls should both stay friendly.*

Green Line 3/4
Vertretungsstunden
ISBN: 978-3-12-560036-2

1 Adjectives

Work in groups or pairs. Cut out the adjective cards and lay them face down on the table. When a person takes a card, he/she acts out the adjective on the card or explains the adjective.

If a person looks *really* happy and smiles a lot, they're probably feeling …

Good.

Not quite. It's the opposite of sad.

aggressive	boring	calm	crazy	excited
grumpy	jealous	kind	loud	nervous
quiet	selfish	shy	slow	wise

2 Funny families

a) *Work in groups. Choose a family and cut out the role cards. Each person should take a card. If there aren't enough people in your group, leave one of the role-play cards out. Now read your family's problem card. Act out your roles and try to sort out the problem. Or think of your own family and problem.*

The Pucks	The Royles	The Squires	The Menzies	Your own family!
You're the tired mum. And you've had a hard day.	You're mum. You want everybody to be happy.	You're mum and you've had a bad day. You're angry.	You're mum, you don't have much money and you're a little crazy.	
You're dad. You don't like too much action and you're poor.	You're dad. And you're crazy – in the nicest way!	You're dad. You're always calm and kind.	You're grandma. You're kind, but you're ill and can't look after yourself.	
You're Jill. You're 10 and you're selfish.	You're Lisa, 14, and jealous of your brothers.	You're Ella, 18, beautiful and you know it.	You're James and you're 17, and you like to party.	
You're Elvis. You're 13 and bored.	You're Phil, 12, and shy.	You're Henry, 15, and you're a little aggressive.	You're Liz, 13. You're a bit grumpy.	
You're the grandpa and you're grumpy.	You're William, 10, and very loud.	You're Samantha, 9, and very funny.	You're Ben, 6, and you think you're the best.	
Problem: Saturday night. Grandpa is visiting and you must all decide what to eat.	Problem: Dad wants to enter a family competition on TV.	Problem: Your cat has brought a mouse into the house, and it's hidden in Ella's shoe.	Problem: You want to go on holiday but there's nobody to look after grandma.	

b) *Act out your role play for the class.*

ISBN: 978-3-12-560036-2

1 Tandem activity: Telephone messages

Read the notes and act out the telephone messages. First act out message 1. Partner A answers the phone and Partner B leaves the message. Partner A writes down the message and Partner B checks it. Then take turns for message 2.

Partner A Message 1	Partner A Message 2
Melde dich. (Hello, this is … Is Ellen there?)	(Hello?) *Sag, dass du gern mit Chris sprechen möchtest.*
Sag, dass Ellen noch in der Schule ist. Frage, ob du ihr etwas ausrichten kannst. (Yes, please. I'm having a party at my house. Ellen can come over around 7 o'clock.)	(I'm afraid he isn't at home now. Can I take a message?) *Sage, dass er dich vor 19.30 zurückrufen soll.*
Frage nach dem Namen und der Adresse des Anrufers. (My name's Bailey and I live in 15, Barton Road.)	(I'll tell him. What's your name and does Chris have your telephone number?) *Du heißt Abigail und deine Telefonnummer ist 0162 549 3425.*

Partner B Message 1	Partner B Message 2
(Hello?) *Sag hallo und frage, ob Ellen da ist.*	*Melde dich.* (Hello, this is … I'd like to speak to Chris, please.)
(Ellen is still at school. Can I take a message?) *Sag, dass du eine Party gibst und Ellen einladen möchtest. Sie kann ab 19.00 vorbeikommen.*	*Sage, dass er nicht da ist und frage, ob du etwas ausrichten sollst.* (Could he call me back before 7.30, please?)
(What's your name and where do you live?) *Sage, dass du Bailey heißt und in der Barton Road 15 wohnst.*	*Frage, wie der Anrufer heißt und ob Chris die Telefonnummer hat.* (My name is Abigail and my phone number is 0162 549 3425.)

2 A play: Messages gone wrong!

a) *Read the short story and complete the grid about the messages.*

Corey calls his parents after school to say that he is going to his friend Taylor's house to do some homework. His parents aren't there and he leaves a message on the answering machine. He's actually going to a party at Ashley's house. Corey calls his friend, Taylor, to tell him what to say if his parents call. Taylor isn't there. Corey leaves a message with his parents to tell Taylor to call him back on his mobile. Taylor gets home and tries to call Corey, but Corey doesn't hear his mobile because it's in his bag. Ashley hears it and answers it. Taylor tells Ashley he wants to speak to Corey and Ashley invites him to the party, too.

Call	Who called?	Who did they speak to?	Who did they want to speak to?	What was the message about?
1	Corey	answerphone		
2				
3				

b) *In groups, decide how the story ends. Write the story as a play and act it out for your class. Decide who is going to be Corey, Taylor, Ashley, Taylor's mum or dad, and Corey's mum or dad.*

ISBN: 978-3-12-560036-2

1 How to help people / Asking for help

Have a look at the following phrases. Underline phrases you can use if you want to help people in green and phrases you can use if you need help in black.

Excuse me, can you …	That's no problem.	I'm sorry, but …
Thank you very much.	That's very kind of you.	Don't worry. I can help you.
Could you … for me?	Never mind.	You've been a great help.
You're welcome.	That's OK.	Can you do me a favour?

2 Tandem activity: How to help people

a) *Cut out these situation cards. Each partner gets one card. Write little dialogues for the situations.*

Situation 1, Partner A

You're Chris, you're 14 years old and you're on your way to school. At the bus station you see an old lady. She looks lost. You ask her if you can help her.

Situation 2, Partner A

You're Kristen, you're 35 years old and you have got a little son, Jason (1 year). You have to go to work in an hour. Now the baby sitter just called and told you that she's ill and can't come. You can't take Jason with you. You go to your neighbour, Miranda, and want to ask her for help. Her daughter Keira, 14, opens the door.

Situation 3, Partner A

You're Steven, you're 15 years old. You met Jasmine at a party and you really liked her. But Jasmine doesn't go to your school and you don't have her telephone number. You ask your friend Mike for help.

Situation 1, Partner B

You're Maureen, you're 77 years old and you want to visit your son who lives in a different city. You arrived by train and now you need to take a bus, but you've forgotten which one. You just know that you need to get off at Lancaster Street.

Situation 2, Partner B

You're Keira, you're 14 years old. You love little children and do babysitting in your free time. You live with your mother, Miranda, in a flat, but your mother isn't at home. Suddenly the doorbell rings. It's Kristen, the neighbour from next door with her little son, Jason. You like Jason very much and want to help her.

Situation 3, Partner B

You're Mike, you're 15 years old and your friend is Steven. You went to a party with him two weeks ago. Steven talked to a girl at the party, Jasmine. You know her because she's a friend of your sister. Now Steven has a problem. Can you help him?

b) *Now choose one scene and act it out to your class.*

3 A new pupil

Simon is a new pupil in Rhona and Shirin's class. He has moved with his family from York to Swansea.

a) *Everything is new for Simon: a new house, a new city, a new school, a new class … and he doesn't know anyone. How does he feel before he goes to his new school for the first time?*

b) *Shirin can understand how Simon feels because she was new in Swansea a year ago. She's thinking about what she and her class could do to make Simon feel welcome. Now think about it yourself and write down at least four of five ideas.*

c) *Decide on one idea and write a dialogue between Shirin, Rhona and Simon.*

Green Line 3/4
Vertretungsstunden
ISBN: 978-3-12-560036-2

Looking at … A Pakistani family

"Where shall I put the photos?" Tariq asked his mum. The boys were still carrying boxes – the family was moving house this weekend and there was still a lot to do. "Oh, the photos," Aunt Zeba said. "Give them to me. Where did you find them? I was looking for them. Thanks Tariq." Tariq gave her the photos and went upstairs to get some more boxes. "Girls," Aunt Zeba said to Shirin and Rhona, "Would you like to see some old family photos?" "That'd be great, Aunt Zeba," Shirin said.

"Here are some very old black and white pictures of your grandparents when they were still in Pakistan." Rhona and Shirin looked at the photos. There was a beautiful, young woman with a beautiful dress. Next to her was a man with a turban[1]. "That's your grandparents' wedding[2] photo," Aunt Zeba told Shirin. "It looks beautiful, but it doesn't look like a wedding dress," Rhona said. "Well, it does," Aunt Zeba replied, "it's a Punjabi wedding dress which is called 'sari'. The women in England wear white dresses for their wedding but in Pakistan they wear saris in colours like red and gold."

"This photo is from 1958. Three years later my father, your grandfather, decided to go to Britain. Life in Pakistan was often very hard and he hoped to earn more money in Britain." "Could he just go over to Britain like that?" Shirin asked. "Well, Pakistan was once a colony of Britain and at that time it was still very easy for the people from the old colonies to come to Britain – the British factories needed workers," Aunt Zeba replied. "Dad wasn't born in Pakistan, was he?" Shirin asked. "No, I was one year old when we arrived in England in 1961. Your uncles weren't born yet. And your father is the baby of the family. He was born in 1970." Shirin had to smile. She thought it was very funny when Aunt Zeba called her father "the baby". "Your grandmother had to stay at home with us children because your grandfather worked long hours. She didn't speak any English at first, that's why we spoke Punjabi at home. When I came to primary school I didn't speak much English. That was very difficult. And now my boys only speak very little Punjabi." "But it's important that they speak English, Aunt Zeba," Shirin said. "You just said how difficult it was for you at school." "Yes, of course, Shirin, you're right. But it would be nice if they spoke Punjabi, too. It's our language and part of our culture." "Mum said that she was really scared when she first visited dad's family," Shirin said. "Oh yes," Aunt Zeba laughed. "I remember that day. It was 1992. Your dad and your mum had met at a restaurant. When your mother visited our family for the first time she was really scared. She thought that our family wouldn't like her because she was English. Some Pakistani families want their sons to marry Pakistani women. But your grandparents liked your mum from the first moment. But I think she was a bit shocked about the big family, and she had never eaten Pakistani food before." "Oh, but now she loves it," Shirin said. "Curries are mum's favourite food." "That's right." Aunt Zeba smiled. "Your mother loves Pakistani food and Pakistani culture. And your mum and dad's wedding in 1995 was a real English-Pakistani wedding." "And then I was born in 1997," Shirin said. "Yes, that's right. Your dad was so proud," Aunt Zeba replied.

"Would you like to move back to Pakistan one day, Aunt Zeba?" Shirin asked. Aunt Zeba looked at her: "No, I wouldn't. Pakistani culture is important for me – it tells me where I come from. But my home is England. And now we have to pack more things. I can't wait to move into my new English-Pakistani home!"

[1] **turban** [ˈtɜːbən] = Turban • [2] **wedding** [ˈwedɪŋ] = Hochzeit

a) *Family history: Read the text and make a timeline. What happened in …*

1958 | 1960 | 1961 | 1970 | 1992 | 1995 | 1997 | today

b) *Have another look at the text and answer these questions. Why …*

… does the wedding photo not look like a wedding photo to Rhona?
… did Shirin's grandfather decide to go to Britain?
… was it quite easy for people from Pakistan to go to Britain at that time?
… does Shirin have to smile when Aunt Zeba talks about her father?
… did Aunt Zeba have a problem when she went to primary school?
… doesn't Aunt Zeba like it that her boys don't speak Punjabi very well?
… was Shirin's mum scared when she first visited her future husband's Pakistani family?
… doesn't Aunt Zeba want to move back to Pakistan?

Green Line 3/4
Vertretungsstunden
ISBN: 978-3-12-560036-2

1 Reading factual texts

Snowdonia National Park in the North of Wales has a great landscape with beautiful mountains. Every year thousands of tourists come here to go hiking and especially to climb Mount Snowdon, the highest mountain in England and Wales. On top of Mount Snowdon you have a great view over Snowdonia National Park. But every year tourists get into trouble because they don't follow important safety rules. There were more than 400 calls for help from hikers and climbers last year on Wales' biggest mountain. For two people the help came too late, and they died.

It's important to plan a Mount Snowdon tour carefully. Tourists should watch the weather forecasts. But keep in mind that temperatures up on the mountain are usually colder than down in the valley[1], and the weather in the mountains can change very quickly. So it's important to take warm clothes like trousers, a hat and a good jacket[2]. It's not a good idea to wear jeans – they dry very slowly. And don't forget good hiking boots! You should also bring some extra food and drink. It's not enough to buy a map and a compass – you also must know how to use them. You should also bring a mobile phone to call for help, but it's even more important that you let people know where you're going. It's a good idea to bring a whistle[3] and a torch[4]; in case of emergency you can make signals and show rescue[5] teams where you are. If you need any advice on mountain safety call the Mountain Rescue at 01690 720333.

[1] **valley** ['væli] = Tal • [2] **jacket** ['dʒækɪt] = Jacke • [3] **whistle** ['wɪsl] = Pfeife • [4] **torch** [tɔ:tʃ] = Taschenlampe, Fackel • [5] **rescue** ['reskju:] = Rettung

a) *Skim the text. What is it about?*

b) *Where can you find information like this? Tick the right answers.*

☐ in a travel guide ☐ in a dictionary ☐ in a sports magazine
☐ in a brochure for outdoor equipment ☐ on the website of the Mountain Rescue team

c) *Write down important mountain safety rules. Use imperative forms.*
Example: Watch the weather forecast before you go.

2 Rhona's adventure in the mountains

This year Rhona's family are spending their holidays in Snowdonia National Park in the North of Wales. This is an e-mail she writes to her friend Shirin.

Dear Shirin,
Dad wanted to get to know the "real Wales" so this year we're spending our holidays in Snowdonia National Park. We're staying at Pen y Pass youth hostel which is close to Mount Snowdon, the highest mountain in England and Wales. Yesterday we wanted to climb it. We started early in the morning. The weather was great so we could just wear jeans and a T-shirt and didn't have to take any jackets. The first part was long but OK. After about two hours mum said: "Shall we go to this lake? It looks so beautiful." But dad said: "No, let's go on. We want to get to the top. This way." So we went on. After a while the path got more dangerous and it was getting really difficult to climb. And mum was getting really angry! Dad said that we must have taken the wrong path and he didn't have a map. We had also forgotten to take our mobiles! But dad said: "Don't worry. When we're at the top there'll be a restaurant and an easy way down. We can even go down on the Snowdon Mountain Railway. Doesn't that sound good?" So we went on. The last part was quite dangerous. There was no path at all and we were wearing only trainers! And it was getting really cold and foggy. When we finally arrived at the top, a big surprise was waiting for us. There was no restaurant, no railway and also no easy way down! It wasn't Mount Snowdon but Crib Goch. We had climbed the wrong mountain!

a) *Which mountain safety rules did Rhona and her family **not** follow?*

b) *How does Rhona's adventure go on? Write an ending to the story.*

Green Line 3/4
Vertretungsstunden
ISBN: 978-3-12-560036-2

Who wants to be a 'Britonaire'?

People in Great Britain are crazy about quizzes. A lot of people go to pub quizzes or table quizzes and play in groups of 4–5. Each team sits at one table and works together. The team with the most correct answers wins. Play this table quiz about Britain in your class.

I Geography (the map in the book might help you)

1. What is the capital of Northern Ireland?

   _ _ _ _ _ _ _

2. Which river runs through Newcastle?

   _ _ _ _

3. What is the name of the highest mountain in Wales?

   _ _ _ _ _ _ _

4. What is the biggest English island?

   _ _ _ _   _ _   _ _ _ _ _

II Famous Britons

Have a look at these faces and write down the name of these famous British people.

____________   ____________

____________   ____________

III Britain in numbers

1. How many people live in the UK?
   a) about 122 million b) about 62 million
   c) about 202 million d) about 92 million
2. How many people fit into Wembley Stadium, London?
   a) 90,000 b) 20,000
   c) 1,000,000 d) 5,000
3. How long is the channel tunnel between England and France?
   a) 100,5 km b) 10,5 km
   c) 50,5 km d) 5,5 km
4. How many kilometres are one mile?
   a) about 1.609 km b) about 0.604 km
   c) about 2.807 km d) about 0.100 km

IV Records

1. Who had six wives?
   a) David Beckham b) King Henry VIII
   c) Prince Charles d) John Lennon
2. The village with the longest name is *Llanfairpwllgwyngyllgogerychwyrndrobwll-llantysiliogogogoch*. Where can you find it?
   a) in Scotland b) in England
   c) in Wales d) in Northern Ireland
3. How high is Ben Nevis, the highest mountain in the UK?
   a) 2,422 metres b) 1,815 metres
   c) 887 metres d) 1,343 metres
4. What is the name of Scotland's biggest pet?
   a) Josie b) Nessie
   c) Rosie d) Lindsay

V Famous Places

Have a look at these places and write down the name.

____________   ____________

____________   ____________

VI Facts

1. What is the name of the British flag?

   _ _ _ _ _   _ _ _ _

2. The national anthem of Great Britain is called:

   God Save the _ _ _ _ _

3. What is the name of a famous pop band from Liverpool?

   _ _ _   _ _ _ _ _ _ _

4. People in Germany pay in euros, people in Britain in …

   _ _ _ _ _ _

Green Line 3/4
Vertretungsstunden
ISBN: 978-3-12-560036-2

Looking at … Soaps in Britain

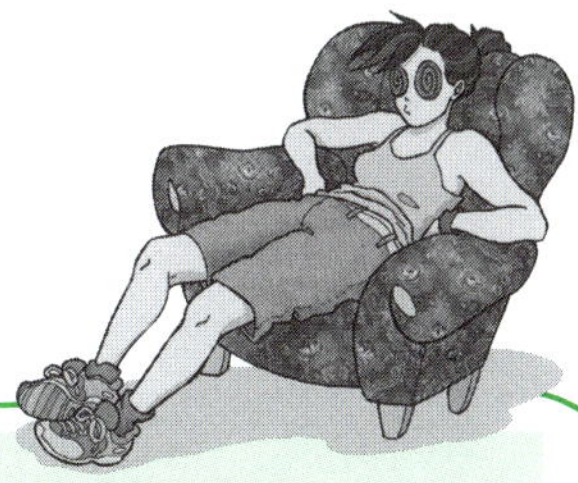

a) *Read about two soaps which are shown regularly in Britain: EastEnders and Neighbours. Match the paragraphs to the right soap and put them in the right order.*

A This soap opera is about people who live in the East End of London. It is filmed by the BBC in their studios in North London. It's shown on the BBC four times a week. It was first shown on British TV on 19th February 1985 and it became very popular very quickly. It is still one of the BBC's most popular programmes. The soap is also shown in many countries around the world, for example the USA and Australia.

B This soap is written mostly for younger people and so it's shown at 6:30 pm. Problems with school and parents are shown and also more serious[1] problems, e. g. with the police or with health. But the soap never stays too serious for long. When the problems become too much, the characters can always get away to the beach. For the makers of the soap the biggest problem is where the soap will go in the future. Will it win the competition with other Australian soaps?

C In 2010 this soap opera was the most popular on British television but it's also the soap opera that creates the most problems for the BBC. It's shown at 7:30 or 8:00 pm in the evening – when young people are watching – but the characters use language and have problems which many people say should *not* be shown to younger people. The BBC have no plans to change anything in the future.

D London's East End is one of the poorer parts of the city, and this can clearly be seen in the soap. The characters in the soap live in small houses or flats and often have money problems. Everything usually happens in their houses, shops and at the pub. The writers of the soap wanted it to show real life and so it often shows real-life problems. One teenage girl had a baby at 15 and some characters have had to go to prison or even die.

E This is an Australian soap opera which was first shown in Australia on 18th March 1985. It is filmed by the Australian company "Ten" in a real street in Melbourne, but it's also sometimes filmed in different parts of Australia and around the world. It was shown in Britain for the first time in 1986 and is now more popular in Britain than in Australia. At first it was shown on BBC One but it is now shown by Channel 5.

F The characters in this soap opera live or work in a part of the city which is definitely not poor. You see the characters in their houses, schools or cafés. Also a lot of the action is outside – in gardens or even on the beach. The writers of the soap wanted to show how young people deal with older people; many young actors have begun their careers in this series. Kylie Minogue, for example, first became famous in this soap.

[1] **serious** ['sɪərɪəs] = ernst

EastEnders: Paragraphs ____________________ Neighbours: Paragraphs ____________________

b) *Complete the grid about the two soap operas.*

	EastEnders	Neighbours
Where is it made?		
Who makes it?		
Where is it shown?		
Storyline		

c) *Find out about a German soap opera and write about it in your exercise book.*

Green Line 3/4
Vertretungsstunden
ISBN: 978-3-12-560036-2

1 Media and more!

a) *Complete the gaps in the two short texts with the correct form of the verb. Use the simple present form of the passive. Then draw lines to match the texts to the things they describe.*

1. It ____________________ (write) by many authors who ____________________ (not; pay). Every day it ____________________ (use) by millions of people all over the world. In this way information ____________________ (share) by people who can use the Internet.
2. These ____________________ (show) every day on most TV channels. They ____________________ (often; do) very cleverly and are fun to watch. It ____________________ (hope) that people will buy the things which ____________________ (show).

The Internet
Ebay
Wikipedia
The Radio
Soaps
Advertisements

b) *Write texts using the passive to describe the other things in 1a). You can also describe other media words. Give your texts to a partner. Can your partner guess what they describe?*

2 Media!

Rewrite the text about computers with the passive. Be careful: Not every sentence can be written in the passive! Use your exercise book. Start like this: The media are used for …

People use the media for information and communication. People know that the Romans used a kind of newspaper thousands of years ago. Men wrote out information in the market place in Rome. Romans read about great battles which Julius Caesar had won. Hundreds of years later they made newspapers and books out of paper.

Plays were also an early form of media. People performed plays in towns all over the world. People watched them for entertainment but also for information. With the invention of television and radio, a much larger audience could get entertainment and information. These new media also informed people more quickly about what happened in other parts of the world.

In the last fifty years modern technology has greatly improved communication. The modern media have changed our whole life. How will new inventions change it in the future?

3 A party for the stars!

a) *Look at the sentences below. Tick the ones in which the verbs have two objects.*

1. ☐ A rich actor sent an invitation to many important directors and actors.
2. ☐ He made wonderful food for his guests.
3. ☐ Some famous pop stars played great music at his party.
4. ☐ At the end of the evening a director offered the rich actor a great role in a new film.
5. ☐ The actor has organised many other parties since then.
6. ☐ In the last few years other directors have promised him good roles.

b) *Rewrite the sentences which you ticked in a) in both forms of the passive (Passive 1 and Passive 2) in your exercise book. Underline the passive form which you think would sound better in a text.*

Green Line 3/4
Vertretungsstunden
ISBN: 978-3-12-560036-2

1 Advertisements

Look at the products below (Partner A and B) and answer these questions. Sort your ideas in a grid.

1. Which people use these products most or go to these places – young or old, men or women?
2. Which adjectives can be used to describe the products or places?
3. What else is often connected with these products or places?

2 Tandem activity: Find the products

a) *Partner B describes his/her ads. Partner A guesses which of his/her products partner B's ads are for.*

b) *Partner A describes his/her ads. Partner B guesses which of his/her products partner A's ads are for.*

c) *Look at the ads with your partner. Do you think they advertise the product well? Why or why not?*

Partner A

Products:

Ad 1:

Ad 2:

Partner B

Products:

Ad 1:

Ad 2:

1 Book Quiz: The media

What do you remember about the media? Choose the right answer to the questions below. Then check your answers in the book.

1. When was the first colour TV made? ☐ 1914 ☐ 1934 ☐ 1954 ☐ 1974
2. When did the BBC start? ☐ 1902 ☐ 1922 ☐ 1942 ☐ 1962
3. What was the first Internet search engine called? ☐ Lycos ☐ Google ☐ Yahoo ☐ Alltheweb
4. When did the Times newspaper start? ☐ 1685 ☐ 1735 ☐ 1785 ☐ 1835
5. Which of these are "popular" newspapers? ☐ The Times ☐ The Sun ☐ The Telegraph ☐ The Daily Mirror
6. Who created the first browser? ☐ Tim Berners-Lee ☐ Bill Gates ☐ Steve Jobs ☐ Steve Wozniak
7. When did the World Wide Web start? ☐ 1961 ☐ 1971 ☐ 1981 ☐ 1991
8. Which British soap has been on TV the longest? ☐ EastEnders ☐ Coronation Street ☐ Neighbours ☐ Emmerdale Farm

2 General knowledge: The Internet!

a) *Can you guess the right numbers? Use the Internet to check your answers.*

1. How many friends does a Facebook user have on average?
2. How many Twitter accounts are there?
3. How many videos are watched on YouTube every day?
4. How many years would you need to live to watch *all* the videos on YouTube?
5. How many articles are there in Wikipedia?
6. How many people use Facebook regularly?
7. How many minutes do people spend on Facebook each visit?
8. What per cent of Internet users read blogs[1]?

b) *Now research the Internet habits[2] of your class. Write questions and give them to the pupils in your class to answer. Examples:*

Do you use Facebook? How often do you download music?

c) *Put the results you got in b) in a grid and present them to your class.*

[1] **blog** [blɒg] = Blog; Internettagebuch • [2] **habit** [ˈhæbɪt] = Gewohnheit

Green Line 3/4
Vertretungsstunden
ISBN: 978-3-12-560036-2

1 On holiday on the Isle of Wight

a) *Match the questions and answers (or comments and replies). Draw lines.*

1. Glen: How long are you staying on the island?
2. Sally: Have you ever been here before?
3. Glen: Where did you go yesterday?
4. Glen: What will the weather be like tomorrow?
5. Glen: Can you go surfing on this island?
6. Sally: Would you like to go surfing with us tomorrow?

Glen: Yes, I came here two years ago.

Sally: Yes, but go to the west of the island if you want to go surfing; the waves are better there.

Sally: We're staying till next Saturday.

Sally: We went to Steephill Cove.

Glen: That'd be great, but I can't surf.

Sally: It will be windy but cold.

b) *Now report the short dialogues from a) in indirect speech. Write them in your exercise book.*

Glen asked how long Sally was staying ...

2 Report a dialogue

Partner work: Choose (part of) a dialogue from the book and report it. Give it to your partner. He/she should give you his/her reported dialogue at the same time. Who can find the original dialogue in the book first?

TIP

Report about 6 lines of dialogue – but don't make it too difficult for your partner!

3 An indirect speech game

Play this game in groups of three or four.

1. Split into groups of three or four.
2. Everybody writes four sentences (questions, statements and commands) on different pieces of paper and reports the sentences on the back of the paper.
3. The groups exchange their sentences.
4. Put the sentences on the table between the group.
5. The first person reads a sentence.
6. The second person should report it.

   If the person reports the sentence correctly, they get the piece of paper and can read the next sentence.

   If they report the sentence incorrectly, the next person can try.
7. The winner is the person who can get the most pieces of paper.

Green Line 3/4
Vertretungsstunden
ISBN: 978-3-12-560036-2

Tandem activity: Small talk openers

a) *Look at the sentences below and split them into "openers" (comments with which you can start a conversation) and responses (comments with which you can continue a conversation). Write the list in your exercise book. (Not all the phrases you see here are as polite as they* ***could*** *be …)*

Partner A

It's a beautiful day today, isn't it?
Er, I don't know. I don't think I know you.
Oh no. I think it's quite warm actually.
The bus is late again. It's typical, isn't it? And then three come at the same time!
Are you on holiday here, too?
Oh, I don't really like it. I don't like techno.

Partner B

Yes, it is. It's been nice for a few days, hasn't it?
What cool music! Do you know who it is?
Oh, I think the buses are quite good in Liverpool.
Yes, I am. We arrived on Saturday.
A bit cold today, isn't it?
Don't I know you from somewhere?

b) *Now practice small talk with a partner:*

1. Partner A: Choose an opener and say it to Partner B.
2. Partner B: Choose a response to Partner A from your list.
3. Partner A and B: Think about the response. Is it polite? Does it show the speaker wants to talk or not?
4. Take turns: Now Partner B starts with an opener.

TIP

Samuel Johnson, who was born 300 years ago, said, "When any two Englishmen meet, their first talk is of the weather." This is still (almost) true today. They don't (usually) start talking about the weather because they are interested in it, but because they want to start a conversation. If you want to carry on talking, you should agree with them.

c) *Look at the pictures below. The people don't know each other. How many different ways can you think of to start a conversation? Write down some sentences in your exercise book. With your partner, choose one of the pictures and start a dialogue.*

1.

2.

3.

4.

d) *Think of a holiday which you didn't like and tell your partner about it. Your partner should show that he/she is interested.*

We went to Italy on holiday last year.

Oh, did you? Did you enjoy it?

Green Line 3/4
Vertretungsstunden
ISBN: 978-3-12-560036-2

Klett

Looking at ... Transport in Britain

a) *Match the texts below to the types of transport they describe.*

Train travel: ___ Coach travel: ___ London Transport: ___ Greater Manchester Transport: ___

A I don't know which website you were looking at but no, you don't need to get a travelcard before you come. The best thing is to get an Oyster card when you get here. You can get them from the station or from newsagents. They cost 5 pounds but you get that back when you give the Oyster card back at the end of your holiday. They're great. You can put some money on your card (like a top-up card for your mobile) and then every time you use it – on the bus or the Tube – the money is taken from your card. It's so much easier than buying a ticket every time you travel! And it's a lot cheaper, too. You can even use them for boat transport on the Thames.
If you want to I could buy one for you before you come. What do you think?

B
AP91: I've just sold my car and I can't work out how the transport system works. Can anyone out there help me?
Peggy7: Just look on the website: tfgm.com and you can find out everything.
Busfan123: In the centre of Manchester you can catch the No. 1 and the No. 2 buses and they're free.
Oldlady: If you're over 60, you can travel free.
EricA40: The Metrolink is great but remember to buy your ticket before you get on the tram!
AP91: There's no Metrolink near me. What about buses?
Busfan123: It's cheapest if you get a return ticket, but you must use the same company[1] for both ways.

C Went to Brighton today. Fantastic. Met Rachel and went to the beach. It only took an hour and it wasn't too expensive because I bought a day return ticket (£22.50). Then I wanted to go home. And that's when the problems started! I'd promised mum I'd be home at 8 pm. Test at school tomorrow!
So I wanted to get the train at 6:17 pm but I missed it. No problem – I thought. But I couldn't get the next train at 6:34 – it was a different train company which I couldn't use with my ticket! I couldn't believe it. I didn't know you had to get different tickets for different companies! I was NOT happy – the man in the ticket office said you can get tickets for all the trains but they're more expensive! So I was late, mum was angry, and now I'm worried about the test tomorrow. Stupid trains!

D

Cheapest fares Manchester to London!

Journey time from 4 hours 30 minutes.

Check out our services to airports.

All coaches have toilets!

[1]**company** ['kʌmpənɪ] = Unternehmen

b) *Match the texts to the types of text below.*

Advertisement: ___ Diary entry: ___ E-mail: ___ Internet chat: ___

c) *Read the statements about the texts and decide if they are true or false.*

	true	false
1. If you buy an Oyster card, you can travel all around London for £5.		
2. There are different train companies in England.		
3. The Metrolink is a bus company in Manchester.		
4. People pay different fares on the coach – it's only cheap if you buy early.		

d) *Rewrite text B as an advertisement. Rewrite text C as an e-mail.*

Green Line 3/4
Vertretungsstunden
ISBN: 978-3-12-560036-2

A look at the map in the front of your book and Kelsey's web album will help you to answer these quizzes.

1 Tandem activity: The 50 states of the US

Give these clues to a partner. He/She has to find out the right state and find it on the map.

Partner A

Give Partner B these clues.

1. It's next to Mexico and home to the Grand Canyon.
2. Its capital Detroit is famous for its car industry.
3. This state is next to Canada. It's very big and cold here.
4. Many tourists visit this US state with its warm weather and its long coast. In its national parks you can even find alligators.
5. New Orleans is the capital of this state which is famous for its jazz music.
6. The Statue of Liberty "lives" in this state.
7. This state is in the South, next to North Carolina and Georgia.
8. This is the youngest of the United States. It's made up of islands and it's in the middle of the Pacific Ocean.

Partner B

Give Partner A these clues.

1. The battle of Wounded Knee took place here.
2. You can find the White House, the home of the US president, here.
3. This is the second biggest US State and it's on the Mexican border[1].
4. Route 66 starts in San Francisco and ends in this state.
5. In this state you can find Hollywood – the centre of the film industry.
6. Yellowstone National Park can be found in this state.
7. This is the biggest state in New England.
8. This state has the same name as its most important city. You can find it on the East Coast.

[1] **border** ['bɔːdə] = Grenze

2 A crossword puzzle

a) *Look at the clues and fill in the crossword puzzle.*

Across
4. highest mountain in the US
5. This part of the US is called the Corn Belt.
6. This ocean can be found on the East Coast of America.
7. a famous national park
8. mountains which go through the states of Wyoming, Colorado and New Mexico

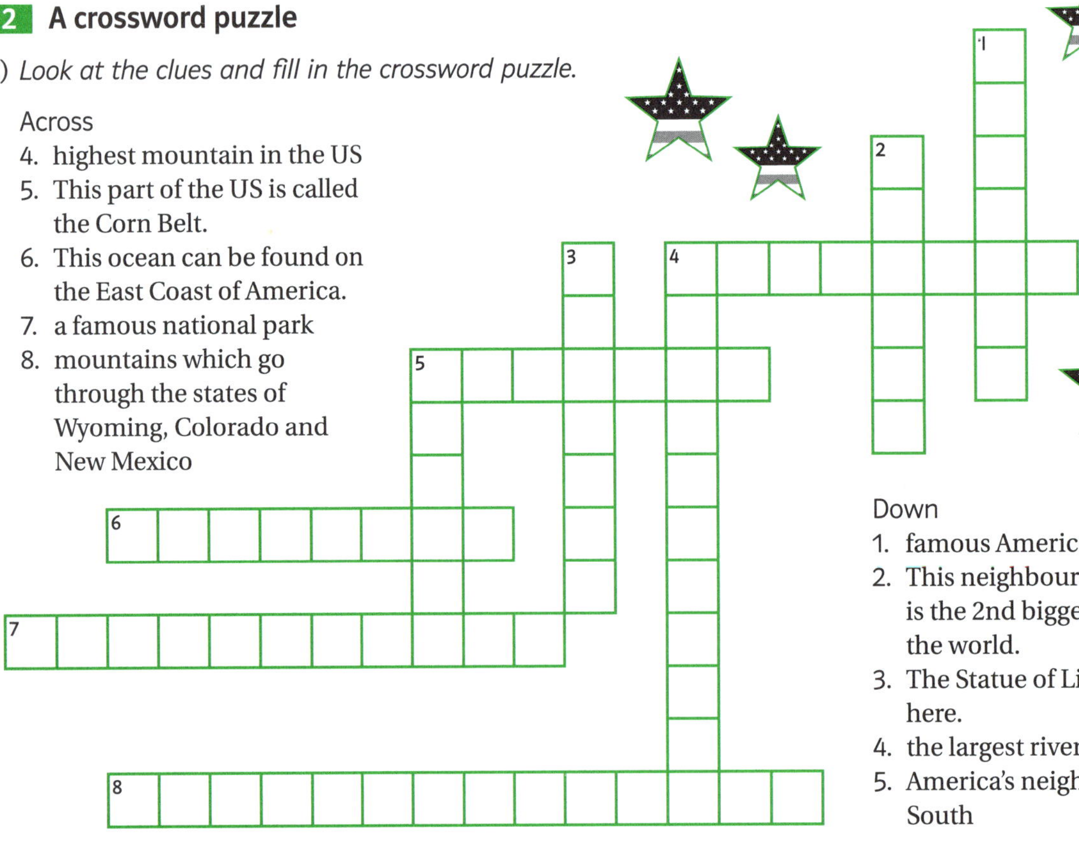

Down
1. famous American highway
2. This neighbour north of the US is the 2nd biggest country in the world.
3. The Statue of Liberty "lives" here.
4. the largest river in the US
5. America's neighbour to the South

b) *Create your own USA crossword puzzle and give it to a partner.*

Green Line 3/4
Vertretungsstunden
ISBN: 978-3-12-560036-2

Tandem activity: New New Yorkers

Jason Davis works for a magazine and he interviews two young people who have come to New York. With a partner, do the interviews. Each of you has to complete his/her question or answer with the right form of the present perfect progressive. Take turns after the first interview.

Partner A
Ana (19) from the Dominican Republic wants to be a musical star.
How long have you been living in New York and why did you come here?
You: I *(to live)* in New York *(for/since)* two months now. I *(to dream)* of becoming a musical star *(for/since)* a long time and I've come to New York to live my dream.
How long have you been dancing?
You: I *(to dance)* ballet *(since/for)* I was four years old and I *(to sing) (for/since)* ten years.
Have you been acting in any big musicals?
You: I *(to go)* to a lot of castings *(for/since)* I arrived. But so far they haven't given me any roles.
What have you been doing for the last months?
You: I *(to live)* in a youth hostel *(for/since)* I arrived and I *(to work)* in a restaurant now *(for/since)* four weeks to pay for the hostel.
Raphael (21) from France wants to be a model.
You: How long *(you/to live)* in New York and why did you come here?
I've been living here for five months now and I came here to work as a model.
You: How long *(you/to work)* as a model?
I've been working as a model for more than two years. But it was easier in France. I've been going to a lot of castings in New York since I arrived. They've been telling me that I should come back and they've been promising me jobs, but so far I've just had one job as a model.
You: What *(you/to do)*, then?
I've been working in a fast food restaurant for two months now, but I hate the job. I've been trying to find a job in a fitness studio or as a personal trainer.
You: Where *(to live) (for/since)* you arrived?
I've been staying with a friend since I arrived. But we've been arguing a lot for the last two months and I need to move out. I've been trying to find a room since July but it's very difficult because New York is so expensive.

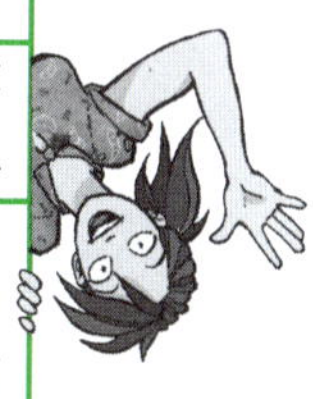

Partner B
Ana (19) from the Dominican Republic wants to be a musical star.
You: How long *(you/to live)* in New York and why did you come here?
I've been living in New York for two months now. I've been dreaming of becoming a musical star for a long time and I've come to New York to live my dream.
You: How long *(you/to dance)*?
I've been dancing ballet since I was four years old and I've been singing for ten years.
You: *(you/to act)* in any big musicals?
I've been going to a lot of castings since I arrived. But so far they haven't given me any roles.
You: What *(you/to do) (for/since)* the last months?
I've been living in a youth hostel since I arrived and I've been working in a restaurant now for four weeks to pay for the hostel.
Raphael (21) from France wants to be a model.
How long have you been living in New York and why did you come here?
You: I *(to live)* here *(for/since)* five months now and I came here to work as a model.
How long have you been working as a model?
You: I *(to work)* as a model *(for/since)* more than two years. But it was easier in France. I *(to go)* to a lot of castings in New York *(for/since)* I arrived. They *(to tell)* me that I should come back and they *(to promise)* me jobs, but so far I've just had one job as a model.
What have you been doing, then?
You: I *(to work)* in a fast food restaurant *(for/since)* two months now, but I hate the job. I *(to try)* to find a job in a fitness studio or as a personal trainer.
Where have you been living since you arrived?
You: I *(to stay)* with a friend *(for/since)* I arrived. But we *(to argue)* a lot *(for/since)* the last two months and I need to move out. I *(to try)* to find a room *(for/since)* July but it's very difficult because New York is so expensive.

Green Line 3/4
Vertretungsstunden
ISBN: 978-3-12-560036-2

Looking at … The Statue of Liberty

a) *The Statue of Liberty has many symbols*[1]. *Look at the pictures, the words and the texts and match them. Use a dictionary if you need help.*

robe | crown | torch | broken chains | law book

a) Prisoners used to have chains around their feet. But these chains are broken. She's free.

b) The statue holds this in her right hand. The light is a symbol of hope.

c) This looks like a dress of the Roman goddess Libertas – which means 'liberty'.

d) This book is the Constitution of the US – the rights of the people.

e) The seven spikes look like the sun (= light) and stand for the seven seas and continents.

[1] **symbol** ['sɪmbl] = Symbol

b) *Put the following paragraphs about the history of the Statue of Liberty in the right order.*

☐ In 1876 Bartholdi travelled to the US to show his idea of the statue to the American people. They were very excited about it the arm alone was about 12 meters long! Bartholdi had also travelled to America to find the right place for the statue. He thought that the harbour of New York was perfect: This was where the people first arrived in the US and it would be the first thing they would see of the New World.

☐ In 1884 Bartholdi and his workers finished the statue. But it was too big to put on a ship and send to the US. The statue's 300 pieces were put into 214 big boxes and sent to New York. But in New York the American people hadn't finished the statue's base[1]! They didn't have enough money and had to raise more before the work could go on. It took another two years until it was finished.

☐ In 1865 a group of French people had the idea to build a statue and give it to the American people as a symbol of their friendship; the French wanted to give the Americans a 'birthday present' for the country's 100th birthday in 1876. But it took a few years longer until the present finally arrived in the US. Auguste Bartholdi wanted to build a statue that looked like a woman. But Bartholdi and the other French people needed a lot of money for their statue because they wanted it to be very big. They asked the French people for money and managed to raise enough for the statue. Bartholdi could finally begin work on the statue.

☐ Bartholdi built his statue with copper, a metal which turns green after some time. But it was too difficult for him to build such a tall statue alone. That's why he asked the engineer Gustave Eiffel for help. (Gustave Eiffel? Have you ever heard of him? Yes, he later built the Eiffel Tower in Paris.) The work on the statue went on, and in 1878 the statue's face was finished and shown at the Paris World Exhibition.

☐ In October 1886, almost ten years after America's 100th birthday, the Statue of Liberty on Liberty Island was given to the American people. With its 93 meters the statue can be seen from a long distance and for a long time it was the first thing many immigrants saw when they arrived in the US. They had come to the US in hope of freedom[2], liberty[3] and a new life – the statue was a symbol of it. Today the Statue of Liberty is an important tourist attraction. You can go to Liberty Island by ferry and climb the 354 steps inside the statue to get to the viewing windows in the crown.

[1] **base** [beɪs]= Fuß, Sockel • [2] **freedom** ['fri:dəm]= Freiheit • [3] **liberty** ['lɪbəti] = Freiheit; Unabhängigkeit

c) *The Statue of Liberty tells her own story:* "Hello, my name is Statue of Liberty. I live in New York but I was born in France. My father was …" *Go on.*

Green Line 3/4
Vertretungsstunden
ISBN: 978-3-12-560036-2

1 Putting feelings into words

a) *Look at these faces.*
Match the feelings to the pictures:

angry | bored | in love | excited

1 ______

2 ______

3 ______

4 ______

b) *Now have a look at these phrases. Which phrase belongs to which emotion?*

- ☐ "I just can't believe it! Isn't it wonderful?"
- ☐ "I'm sorry, I wasn't listening. What did you say?"
- ☐ "I know that! You don't have to tell me!"
- ☐ "You're a wonderful person!"
- ☐ "He's absolutely fantastic!"
- ☐ "Don't do that again!"
- ☐ "What's the time?"
- ☐ "It's fantastic!"
- ☐ "He's so sweet!"

2 Idiomatic English

a) *On the left you find typical English idioms[1] which express emotions. Try to guess what they mean. Draw lines the correct sentences on the right.*

"He feels like a fish out of water!"	He's absolutely happy about something.
"He feels on top of the world!"	He feels uncomfortable in a situation.
"He really needs to let off steam!"	He's very excited and can't sit still.
"He's got ants in his pants!"	He's in love with someone and can't think of anything else.
"He's head over heels in love!"	He's very happy with himself, e. g. because he has won a competition.
"He's proud as a peacock!"	He's so hungry he could eat anything.
"He could eat a horse!"	He's angry or aggressive about something and needs to say or do something to get his mind off it.

[1] **idiom** ['ɪdiəm] = Redewendung

b) *Try to think of situations which are typical of the idioms.*

Example: You might feel like a fish out of water at a football stadium because you can't stand football.

3 Emotions, emotions, emotions

a) *Samantha calls her friend Gemma to tell her about something which happened to her. How does Samantha feel? Underline typical words and phrases in which she shows her feelings.*

"Hi Gemma. This is Sam. Something fantastic happened today! I have to tell you! You won't believe it. There's this boy from my sports club, Wayne. He's really nice. And he's cute, but I didn't think he even knew who I was. Today I met him on the bus. He was sitting in the back row. I didn't get a seat but I stood next to him. I said 'Hi'. He looked at me and said: 'Ah, I know you. You're in the judo club.' He'd forgotten my name but he knew who I was. Isn't that great? He knew who I was!!! And then we talked about judo and everything. But then guess what happened? All of a sudden the bus suddenly stopped and I fell onto him! Oh my God! It was so embarrassing! I think my head turned red. But he was so nice. He just laughed and smiled at me. I had to get off at the next stop but just before I left he said: 'Would you like to go to the movies with me tomorrow afternoon? There's a fantastic new movie about judo.' Wow, isn't that great! He wants to go to the movies with me. I can't believe it!"

b) *Now rewrite the text in a different emotion (e.g. sad). Change words and phrases, and change what has happened as well. Can your partner guess the emotion(s)?*

Green Line 3/4
Vertretungsstunden
ISBN: 978-3-12-560036-2

A guided bus tour through New York

a) *You and your parents are in New York. You're taking part in a guided bus tour in English. Your parents don't speak English very well so you have to tell them what the tour guide is saying. Tell the guide your parents' questions, too. You don't need to translate word for word.*

Guide: Hi, everybody, and welcome to our bus tour of New York. My name is Richard Wood and I'll be your guide today.
We start our tour here at Brooklyn Bridge which connects[1] the New York boroughs of Brooklyn on the other side of the bridge and Manhattan over here. It opened in 1883 and so the Brooklyn Bridge is one of the oldest suspension bridges[2] in the US.

You: …

Deine Eltern wollen wissen, wie viele Stadtteile New York hat.

You …

Guide: Brooklyn and Manhattan are just two of the five New York boroughs. The others are Queens, the Bronx and Staten Island. Manhattan is the oldest borough of New York. Let's have a look around it. Please follow me.

You: …

Guide: New York has a long history of immigration. 36 % of the 8,000,000 New Yorkers were born outside the US and come from many different countries. I think you can guess where the people come from who live in this part of New York.
Yes, we're in Chinatown. Have a look at the beautiful buildings, try some Chinese food at one of the restaurants or take aways, or go and visit one of the Buddhist temples[3]. Chinatown is the biggest community of Chinese people outside China.

You: …

Deine Eltern wollen wissen, wann die ersten chinesischen Immigranten in die USA kamen.

You: …

Guide: The first Chinese immigrants came to the US in the 1850s when gold was discovered in California. But most of the Chinese came here after the Second World War. Even today a lot of Chinese still come to the US.

You: …

Guide: Now we're in Greenwich Village or "the Village" as New Yorkers call this part of the city. It's an old part of town and even today it looks a bit like a village with all the old five- and six-storey buildings and hardly any skyscrapers. In the 1950s a lot of artists and students moved to the Village. Today, the Village is too expensive for many of them and they've moved to other parts of the city.

You:

Deine Eltern wollen wissen, wo die Künstler heute in New York leben.

You: …

Guide: A lot of artists live in Soho, another very interesting part of the city. You can also find a lot of art galleries there.

You: …

Guide: Now we are at the intersection[4] of Fifth Avenue and 34th street. By the way – it's really easy to find your way around NYC because it's like a grid. This is the famous Empire State Building. It's got 102 storeys and is 443 meters tall. It was completed in 1931 and was the tallest building in the world for 40 years until the World Trade Center was built in the 1970s.

You: …

Deine Eltern wollen wissen, was das höchste Gebäude in New York heute ist.

You: …

Guide: After the attacks on the World Trade Center, the Empire State Building again became the tallest skyscraper in New York. But when One World Trade Center is built, it will be the city's tallest building.

You: …

[1]**to connect** [kə'nekt] = verbinden • [2]**suspension bridge** [sə'spenʃən ˌbrɪdʒ] = Hängebrücke • [3]**temple** ['tempəl] = Tempel • [4]**intersection** [ˌɪntə'sekʃən] = Kreuzung

b) *The guide also takes you to Times Square and Central Park. Be the guide. Try to find out information about these places and continue the guided tour.*

c) *Have a look at the map at the back of your English book. Where did you go on your tour?*

Green Line 3/4
Vertretungsstunden
ISBN: 978-3-12-560036-2

Friends

a) *Read the text from Dylan's diary and underline all the examples of the perfect infinitive in green. Then read it again and underline all examples of the passive infinitive in black.*

OK, OK. Maybe I should have invited Glenda to the movies on Friday. But she's always so jealous. I wouldn't have been able to talk to Allison at all. And why shouldn't I go out with Allison? She's just a friend! I'm not married to Glenda, but she always wants to be told about everything I do. She expects to be asked, too, wherever I go. She even comes to baseball practice with me! It's too much. She must be told: I'm a free man and we're not married! But how did she find out anyway? Phil must have told her. How could he have been so mean? He must have known that she'd go crazy. I'll have to call her. And she'll probably expect to be given a nice present or something. Girls! I'm better off without them.

b) *Now read Glenda's thoughts and write sentences with the perfect infinitive and the correct modal.*

Dylan ______________________________ with Allison.

He ______________________________ that I would find out.

He ______________________________ about me, though: I don't mind.

c) *Now read Glenda's conversation with Aileen and write sentences with the passive infinitive.*

Aileen: Yes, well. Dylan's very sweet, but I must say: He isn't a cool dude.

______________________________: Dylan isn't a cool dude.

Glenda: No, he even wants me to cheer for him at baseball practice.

No, he even ______________________________ for at baseball practice.

Aileen: But why did you say yes when Joe asked you out?

Glenda: I was just so surprised. I wasn't expecting it.

I was just so surprised because ______________________________.

Aileen: You should tell Dylan. Somebody might see you with Joe.

Dylan ______________________________. You

______________________________ with Joe.

Glenda: Oh no. I don't think I need to tell him everything. He can't expect that.

Oh no. I ______________________________ to tell him everything.

Green Line 3/4
Vertretungsstunden
ISBN: 978-3-12-560036-2

When should British teenagers be allowed to drive?

a) *Read the text and put the paragraphs in the right order.*

A On the other hand it should be understood why young people are more likely[1] to have accidents than older people. It is partly because they have less experience as they haven't driven as long. If they learnt to drive when they were younger, they would become better at driving sooner. Also, if teenagers learnt to drive when they were still at home, their parents would be able to help them become careful drivers. When teenagers are allowed to be more independent, they behave more like intelligent adults, too.

B First and most importantly, it is well-known that more young drivers have accidents than older drivers. In 2009, for example, 26% of all accidents involved[2] young drivers (aged from 17 to 24). Young drivers have less experience than older drivers and so they have more accidents. Young people also take risks more often than older people. In cars these risks can kill other people.

C Teenagers should not be allowed to get their driver's license[3] until they are 17.

D In conclusion we know that driving on roads is dangerous, but children and young people have to do many things that are dangerous. I believe that teenagers should be able to get their driver's license when they are 16, so that they can learn to drive well sooner.

E Next, we should also ask ourselves if we want more cars on the road anyway. In Britain we have problems with the environment[4] and problems with overweight teenagers. People drive to shops when they could walk, cycle or take the bus. Teenagers don't need to be able to drive; they should use their legs. If people are allowed to drive when they are younger, they will get even less exercise, and there will be even more problems with our environment.

F Fifty years ago children became independent of their parents in Britain when they were 21. Soon after that the age changed and children became adults officially when they were 18. That is still true today. But although people are only seen as adults when they are 18, they are allowed to do many things earlier. Also, in many countries the laws are different, so the question is: When should teenagers be allowed to do what?

G Also, the law doesn't make sense. If British children have to cycle on the road, why should teenagers not be allowed to drive on it? It is well-known that cycling is very dangerous and many people die in bike accidents every year, but still the law allows children to cycle on the road. Surely, if they are expected to cycle, they should also be allowed to drive.

[1] **likely** ['laɪkli] = wahrscheinlich • [2] **to involve** [ɪn'vɒlv] = einschließen • [3] **driver's license** *(AE)* ['draɪvəz ˌlaɪsns] = Führerschein • [4] **environment** [ɪn'vaɪərnmənt] = Umwelt

Order: __ __ __ __ __ __ __

b) *Find the following words or phrases in the text.*

1. a phrase which contrasts something: ______
2. two words which add information: ______
3. two words and one phrase which put things in order: ______
4. two words which give a reason: ______

c) *Choose one of the topics below and write your own argumentative text.*

"Children should be allowed to leave school when they are 14."

"It's always a good thing to be tidy."

TIP
Look at page 40 in your textbook.

Green Line 3/4
Vertretungsstunden
ISBN: 978-3-12-560036-2

1 Students shouldn't have to do sport at school after they're 16

a) *Look at the following sentences and sort them into arguments for and against the above title. Use a grid in your exercise book.*

You can drop other subjects, so why not sport?

It's important to be fit in body and mind.

There are too many people who are overweight.

When you leave school, you don't have to do sport anymore.

It's been shown that sport helps you to think better, too.

You don't have to do sport to stay fit.

Lots of things are good and important, but you can't do everything. There just isn't enough time.

b) *Have a polite discussion with a partner. The phrases for presenting arguments and disagreeing on page 36 will help you.*

Partner A: You are **for** sport at school. First think of more arguments to add to the list then start the discussion by presenting your most important argument.

Partner B: You are **against** sport at school. Think of more arguments to add to the list. Reply to your partner's points and add your own arguments.

c) *Now try an impolite discussion!*

Partner B: You are **for** sport at school. Start the discussion with one of the arguments above.

Partner A: You are **against** sport at school. Disagree with your partner, but you needn't be polite.

d) *In groups, talk about how you felt in each of the discussions.*

"In the impolite discussion I didn't listen to my partner as much."

2 School improvements

a) *In small groups, think of the way you could improve school life most.*

I think it would be better if we started later.

I don't think homework should be allowed.

b) *Then each group should explain their idea to the class, and the class should try and agree on the best idea.*

Green Line 3/4
Vertretungsstunden
ISBN: 978-3-12-560036-2

Tandem activity: All's well that ends well[1]?

Partner A

a) *Sit back to back with Partner B. You both have pictures of a picture story, but you mustn't look at your partner's pictures. You have pictures 1, 3, 5 and 7 in the correct order. Your partner has the other missing pictures, but they're in the wrong order. Look at your pictures and describe them to your partner. Then listen to your partner. Find the correct order for all the pictures.*

1.

3.

5.

7.

b) *Look at the pictures with your partner and write the story as a short story or as a film script. Think about these questions:*

- What happened first?
- How did the man and woman get into that situation?
- What was their relationship?
- What happened at the end?
- Was the woman still alive?
- Did they become friends again?

Partner B

a) *Sit back to back with Partner A. You both have pictures of a picture story, but you mustn't look at your partner's pictures. You have pictures 2, 4, 6 and 8, but they're in the wrong order. Your partner has the other pictures in the right order. Listen to your partner. He/She must describe his/her pictures first. Then describe your pictures to your partner. Find the correct order.*

A

B

C

D

b) *Look at the pictures with your partner and write the story as a short story or as a film script. Think about these questions:*

- What happened first?
- How did the man and woman get into that situation?
- What was their relationship?
- What happened at the end?
- Was the woman still alive?
- Did they become friends again?

[1] **All's well that ends well** [ˈɔːls wel ðət‿endz wel] = Ende gut, alles gut.

Green Line 3/4
Vertretungsstunden
ISBN: 978-3-12-560036-2

1 Revision: Passive or active voice

Have a look at the grid and fill in the missing active and passive sentences or tenses.

active	passive	tense
They produce crisps in this factory.	Crisps are produced in this factory.	Simple present
She's taking the dog for a walk.		Present progressive
	She was hit by a bus while she was crossing the road.	
The band was playing a beautiful song when we came in.		
	The house will be built next summer.	
They haven't caught the burglars yet.		Present perfect
	The computer had been stolen (by two thieves).	

2 A very special lady

Turn these phrases into passive constructions. Can you guess who this very special lady is?

1. Christopher discovered her in the 15th century.

2. White people took her land.

3. People from Mexico call her the El Dorado.

4. Since 2008 her first black president has governed her.

5. France gave her a big statue as a present for her 100th birthday.

Green Line 3/4
Vertretungsstunden
ISBN: 978-3-12-560036-2

Pocahontas

You have probably heard the name Pocahontas, the beautiful Native American princess. There are books about her and in 1995 Walt Disney made a film about her. But did she really exist? Who was she? Read the text and find out.

No one today knows when exactly she was born, but it must have been around 1595.

Pocahontas was one of the many daughters of the Native American chief[1] Powhatan. Her father was the chief of many Native American tribes that lived on the eastern coast of America – which is today the state of Virginia. In fact Pocahontas wasn't her real name; in her tribe she was called Matoaka. In 1607 when Matoaka was probably about eleven or twelve years old, a group of strangers[2] arrived in Chesapeake Bay where Matoaka and her tribe lived. These strangers were the first English colonists[3] who came to live in America. They had sailed all the way from England and now wanted to live on the new continent. They hoped to find gold, silver and other goods which they wanted to bring back to England. They also wanted to bring the Christian[4] religion to the Native Americans and turn them into Christians. They built a new city – Jamestown. But life was very hard on the new continent. The strangers didn't know how to grow fruits and vegetables and many became ill or died of hunger.

The Native Americans and the new settlers didn't always get along well with each other. In 1608 the Native Americans caught one of the colonists, John Smith. Smith was brought to Pocahontas' father Powhatan who wanted him to die. John Smith later wrote that Pocahontas had saved his life, but no one knows whether this is true. He was finally allowed to return to his own people and during the next few years, Pocahontas and other women from the tribe visited them in Jamestown and brought them food. But in 1609 Smith had to return to England and the situation between Native Americans and settlers got worse.

In 1613 the settlers took Pocahontas as a hostage[5]. However, they treated her well. Pocahontas became a Christian and was called Rebecca by the colonists. In Jamestown Pocahontas met John Rolfe and fell in love with him. Rolfe was a farmer from England and he and Pocahontas got married in 1614. It was probably the first marriage[6] between an English colonist and a Native American woman. Pocahontas was now called Rebecca Rolfe. In 1615 their son Thomas Rolfe was born. The following year, the family was invited to come to England. Pocahontas was probably the first Native American woman who ever visited England. The people there were fascinated[7] by her because they had never seen a Native American woman before. The Rolfes were invited to dinner parties and dances, and Pocahontas was painted by famous artists. She even met the King and Queen. In 1617, when the Rolfes wanted to travel back to America, Pocahontas became seriously ill. In March 1617 she died at the age of 21. Her husband returned to America, but her son Thomas stayed in England and went to school there. He returned to America at the age of 20.

Although Pocahontas' life was short, she is remembered because she helped to keep the peace between the colonists and the Indians, and she was probably the first Native American woman to live in Europe.

[1] **chief** [tʃiːf] = Häuptling • [2] **stranger** ['streɪndʒə] = Fremde/-r • [3] **colonist** ['kɒlənɪst] = Kolonist • [4] **Christian** ['krɪstʃən] = Christ/-in, christlich • [5] **hostage** ['hɒstɪdʒ] = Geisel • [6] **marriage** ['mærɪdʒ] = Ehe • [7] **fascinated** ['fæsɪneɪtɪd] = fasziniert

a) *Answer the following questions.*

1. Who was Pocahontas?
2. Who was captured in 1608?
3. What was her name after she became a Christian and got married?
4. When and why did she meet the first white people?
5. To whom did Pocahontas get married?
6. When did she go to England?
7. Why were the people in England fascinated by her?

b) *Write a profile of Pocahontas. Use the information in the text (name, year of birth, family …)*

c) *Imagine you are Pocahontas and you are in England. You are the first Native American woman who has ever been there. Write a letter back home and write about your life in England.*

Green Line 3/4
Vertretungsstunden
ISBN: 978-3-12-560036-2

Klett

Looking at … Polite language

a) *Look at these speech bubbles. Underline polite phrases in green and impolite phrases in black.*

No, I don't want to go. I'm tired.

I'm not talking to you. Shut up.

Would you like to sit over here?

I'm sorry for taking up your time.

No, I didn't say that. You weren't listening.

Get out of my way.

Did you have a good day?

Isn't it a nice day today?

Turn off your phone. It's giving me a headache.

Thanks for helping me.

I don't want that one. I want a bigger piece.

How are you doing?

Nice to meet you.

Would you like to drink something?

That sounds wonderful to me.

I don't have any time now. Come back later.

b) *Now try to turn the impolite phrases into polite ones.*

c) *Look at the German tourists in these pictures. They're in America and they all have a problem and need help. Turn their thoughts into polite phrases/questions.*

1.

2.

3.

4.

d) *What do the Americans answer? Write down little dialogues for these scenes.*

e) *Choose one of the situations and act it out with your partner.*

Green Line 3/4
Vertretungsstunden
ISBN: 978-3-12-560036-2

Mediation: Karl May

An American exchange student visits you and your family. In the newspaper you find an article about Karl May. Your American friend wants to know what it's about.

a) *Tell your friend what the article is about. Don't translate word by word, but tell your exchange partner who Karl May was, what he did, why he became famous, what kind of life he had and what kind of problems he had in life.*

Vom **Taschendieb** zum **Bestsellerautor**

Für die einen war er ein Dieb, für die anderen ein großer Schriftsteller, der mit seinen Büchern ganze Generationen von Jugendlichen begeisterte. Doch wer war dieser Autor wirklich?

Geboren wurde Karl May am 25. Februar 1842 in Ernstthal in **Sachsen**. Seine Eltern waren arm und Karl war das fünfte von 14 Kindern, doch viele seiner Geschwister starben sehr früh. Karl war insofern der einzige Sohn der Familie und seine Eltern wollten, dass er ein besseres Leben haben sollte als sie. Karl wollte Lehrer werden und begann sein Studium in Waldenburg.

Doch Karl stahl immer wieder Dinge, zunächst nur ein paar Kerzen, später eine **Taschenuhr**. 1861 musste er seinen Beruf als Lehrer deswegen aufgeben. Doch auch in den folgenden Jahren wurde Karl immer wieder wegen Diebstählen erwischt und wurde 1865 zu einer 4-jährigen **Haftstrafe** verurteilt.

1874 begann May für Zeitschriften zu schreiben. Er schrieb auch Geschichten und längere Bücher. Gut leben konnte er davon jedoch nicht – immer wieder hatte er hohe **Schulden**.

Erst viel später, im Alter von 50 Jahren, wurde Karl May wirklich erfolgreich. 1892 wurde „Karl Mays gesammelte Reiseromane" veröffentlicht. Diese Bücher machten Karl May berühmt und zum ersten Mal in seinem Leben musste er sich um Geld keine Sorgen mehr machen.

In diesen gesammelten Reiseromanen erschienen auch drei Bände über Karl Mays berühmtesten Helden: Winnetou. Nun spielten seine Bücher im amerikanischen Westen und erzählten vom Leben der Indianer dort und ihren Begegnungen mit den Weißen. Der Held seiner Romane war der Indianerhäuptling Winnetou, der als Häuptling der **Apachen** mit seiner „Silberbüchse" für Frieden und Gerechtigkeit kämpfte. Sein alter Freund und **Blutsbruder** Old Shatterhand, ein Weißer, half ihm dabei.

Schon als Kind war May begeistert von den Geschichten, die die Männer, die aus Amerika zurückkehrten, von dort berichteten. Nun begeisterte er selbst Generationen von Jugendlichen mit seinen Büchern. Dabei war er selbst nie in Amerika gewesen. Erst 1908, vier Jahre vor seinem Tod und 16 Jahre nachdem seine Reiseromane veröffentlicht worden waren, fuhr er zusammen mit seiner Frau Klara nach Amerika und besichtigte dort Albany, Buffalo und die Niagarafälle. Seine Erlebnisse verarbeitete er in dem letzten Buch über den Häuptling der Apachen – Winnetou 4.

Karl May begeisterte mit diesen Büchern viele junge Leser. Doch am meisten begeistert von seinen Büchern war Karl May selbst. Mit der Zeit fiel es ihm schwer, zwischen seinen Büchern und der **Realität** außerhalb der Bücher zu unterscheiden. Er hielt sich selbst für Old Shatterhand und behauptete, die Inhalte seiner Bücher selbst erlebt zu haben. In Radebeul in Sachsen ließ er sich ein großes Haus, „Villa Shatterhand", bauen und er ließ sich vom **Schmied** ein Gewehr anfertigen, das der Silberbüchse von Winnetou in seinem Roman glich. Im Jahr 1912 starb Karl May im Alter von 70 Jahren. Seine Bücher finden bis heute eine große **Anhängerschaft**.

b) *Without a dictionary, explain the meaning of the marked words to your exchange partner (your partner in the classroom).*

Example: Taschendieb: "This is someone who steals. He doesn't steal big things – only small things such as handbags or purses."

Green Line 3/4
Vertretungsstunden
ISBN: 978-3-12-560036-2

Looking at … Canyonlands National Park

Visit CANYONLANDS for the experience of a lifetime

Canyonlands is less known than other national parks in the US and therefore has fewer visitors than some of the more popular parks. Yellowstone has, for example, more than 2 million tourists every year; Canyonlands about 440,000 visitors. If you want to get away from it all and discover what the US was like hundreds of years ago, this is the place for you. It is also great for outdoor enthusiasts, and for people who love the colours of the desert.

Canyonlands is quite a new national park and was only created in 1964 (Yellowstone in 1872). It is a large area, split into four parts, where the Colorado and the Green Rivers meet in Utah. The weather is hot and dry with very little rain, with temperatures which are often over 30°C in summer. The park covers some of the least-visited areas in the US, and there are no roads between the different parts of the park. To visit large areas of the park you need a four-wheel drive or you have to travel on foot or by bike, taking the trails through the canyons. There are no shops in the park, but you can buy water at some of the visitors' centers.

Most visitors travel to the Island in the Sky area which is the easiest to get to. There is a visitors' center there and it's possible to go on hikes which only take a few hours. You can also go on walks together with park rangers. Camping is allowed at one of the official campsites, but only two cars and ten people at the most are allowed to stop at each one.

You can go climbing in the canyons, horse-riding along the trails or canoeing on the rivers. Canoeing is safe enough for the average canoeist on either of the rivers above their confluence, but only experienced canoeists should try canoeing on the water after the two rivers have met, as the river there becomes dangerously fast.

Another interesting part of the park is Horseshoe Canyon, where you can see paintings done over 3,000 to 4,000 years ago. These are some of the oldest paintings ever discovered in the United States. It should be remembered, however, that any paintings of horses must have been painted later, as there were no horses in North America 3,000 or 4,000 years ago.

a) *Read the text about Canyonlands National Park.*
Are the statements below true or false?

	true	false
1. Not many people visit large areas of the park because it is difficult to travel around.		
2. You are allowed to camp anywhere in the park if there are fewer than two cars together.		
3. Canoeing is only safe for experienced canoeists.		
4. Native Americans did not ride horses 4,000 years ago.		

b) *Find words or phrases which mean the following:*

1. a person who loves life outdoors ______________________
2. a kind of jeep which can travel off-road easily ______________________
3. something which is not very good and not very bad ______________________
4. the place where two rivers meet ______________________

c) *Now write a short summary of the park in German for a friend who doesn't speak English.*

Green Line 3/4
Vertretungsstunden
ISBN: 978-3-12-560036-2

1 Gerund or infinitive

Look at the verbs. Which verbs are followed by an infinitive, which are followed by a gerund construction, which verbs can be followed by an infinitive **or** *gerund? Make a grid with three headlines: 'infinitive', 'gerund' and 'both forms' and write the words under the right headline.*

to like | to stop | to begin | to want | to decide

to imagine | to enjoy | to look forward to | to dream of

to hate | to love | to forget | to remember | to try | to dislike

2 Tandem activity: Talk about yourselves

Cut out the cards below. Read the verbs to your partner. He/She has to make a question with them (check the correct form – it's on your card). Now you must give the answer to the question, and give reasons for your answer. Your partner takes the next card and you make the next question, and he/she gives the answer.

Example: **dream of + travel to the US:** "Do you dream of travelling to the US?" –"Yes, I do. I think the US is a great country and I dream of travelling to New York one day. I think it's a great city and I would love to see the Statue of Liberty."

to dream of + travel to the US *(Do you dream of travelling to the US?)*	to enjoy + cook *(Do you enjoy cooking?)*	to imagine + work as a pilot or stewardess *(Can you imagine working as a pilot or stewardess?)*	to try + do bungee jumping *(Have you ever tried to do bungee jumping?)*
to look forward to + finish school *(Do you look forward to finishing school?)*	to want + be a big star *(Do you want to be a big star?)*	to remember + brush your teeth *(Do you always remember to brush your teeth?)*	to dislike + go to school *(Do you dislike going to school?)*
to try + dye your hair *(Have you ever tried to dye your hair?)*	to hate + get up early *(Do you hate getting up early?)*	to begin + study before a test *(When do you usually begin to study before a test?)*	to stop + go to school + if you could *(Would you stop going to school if you could?)*
to dream of + ??? *(Do you dream of + gerund?)*	to imagine + ??? *(Can you imagine + gerund?)*	to enjoy + ??? *(Do you enjoy + gerund?)*	to try + ??? *(Have you ever tried + infinitive?)*
to look forward to + ??? *(Do you look forward to + gerund?)*	would like + ??? *(Would you like + infinitive)*	to want + ??? *(Do you want + infinitive?)*	to hate + ??? *(Do you hate + gerund or infinitive ?)*

Green Line 3/4
Vertretungsstunden
ISBN: 978-3-12-560036-2

Klett

1 A trip to a national park

a) *Rewrite the marked clauses with an infinitive construction.*

When I saw the bear I didn't know **what I should do**.

When I saw the bear I didn't know what ______________________________.

I wasn't sure whether **I should run or stand still**.

I wasn't sure whether ______________________________.

I must be the only person **who tried to talk to a bear**.

I must be the only person ______________________________.

But I wasn't expecting **that the bear would reply**.

But I wasn't expecting ______________________________.

b) *Now translate these sentences with the help of infinitive constructions.*

Ich wollte, dass eine Gruppe Freunde mit mir zum Yellowstone Park kommt.

I wanted a group of friends ______________________________.

Ich habe mich gefragt, wie viele Freunde ich mitnehmen soll.

I wondered how many ______________________________.

Am Ende war Ellie die einzige Person, die ja sagte.

In the end Ellie was the only ______________________________.

Niemand erwartete, dass wir als mehr als gute Freunde zurückkommen würden.

Nobody expected ______________________________.

2 Act a sentence

a) *Group work: In pairs, choose a sentence below and act it out. You can speak, but you mustn't use the words in the sentence. The other pairs should guess which sentence you were acting out. The first pair to guess gets a point. The pair with the most points is the winner.*

- They were climbing a mountain when they stopped to take a photo.
- They stopped taking photos when a rock fell down the mountain and almost hit them.
- He'd meant to check if there was a hole in the canoe before they left.
- They wanted to get back to the camp quickly but that meant carrying the canoe up the hill.
- When we saw the bear, we just went on walking.
- It was a great day. We saw a bear and then went on to walk twenty miles.
- He tried to call his dad, but his mobile wasn't working.
- He tried calling his dad, but his dad couldn't help them either.
- They didn't remember to take the trail which led to the left.
- They remembered walking up the trail which took them to the top of the cliff. What a great day!

b) *When you have acted out the above sentences, everybody should write their own sentences with a gerund or an infinitive.*

Green Line 3/4
Vertretungsstunden
ISBN: 978-3-12-560036-2

1 American or British English?

Find fifteen words in the wordsearch and write them in a grid under the headings AE or BE as below. Then complete the grid with the American or British equivalent and the German translation.

AE	BE	German

B	A	P	A	R	T	M	E	N	T
R	U	B	B	I	S	H	J	P	L
S	T	C	E	N	T	R	E	C	X
W	U	T	H	I	G	H	W	A	Y
E	M	M	O	B	I	L	E	B	F
E	N	Q	B	I	L	L	L	S	R
T	S	U	B	W	A	Y	R	T	I
S	R	A	I	L	W	A	Y	O	E
O	P	A	N	T	S	U	T	R	S
V	H	O	L	I	D	A	Y	E	E

2 A crossword

Complete the crossword.

1. They would remember that day forever. It was …
2. The trail was very … There wasn't enough room for two people to walk side-by-side.
3. That film isn't scary. It's too … You always know what's going to happen.
4. You need some … in yourself to climb that cliff – it's no good if you're nervous.
5. Somebody who takes too many risks is …
6. When you … something, you finally understand it without anybody telling you.
7. Trees are tall, and rivers are … – the water goes down a long way.
8. A … is a person who kills animals in forests, for example, when they aren't allowed to.
9. When you leave school before you pass your exams, you … early.
10. A … is a small path which usually is quite long.
11. A … is a book which tells a story.
12. If you don't think or care about other people or animals, you are …

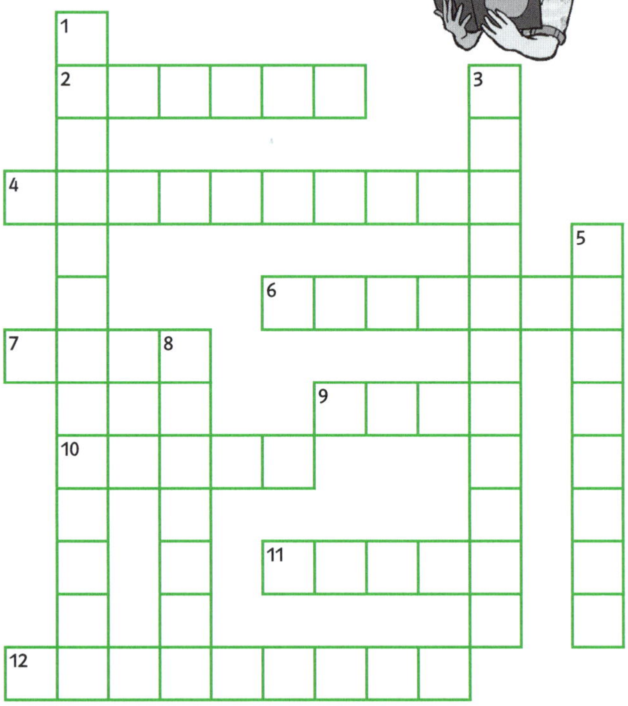

3 Word families

How many words do you know in these word families? Write them down in your exercise book.

end | camp | care | help | usual | fear | back | beauty

TIP
You can use compound nouns, too.

Green Line 3/4
Vertretungsstunden
ISBN: 978-3-12-560036-2

Hollywood stars

Read these texts about famous stars.

a) *Fill in the correct relative pronouns and underline the relative clauses. Put commas where necessary.*

b) *Can you guess who the stars are?*

This English actor ______ also worked as a model, musician and producer, was born in London in 1986. He had already acted in two movies when he played the role of Cedric Diggory in the fourth Harry Potter movie "The Goblet of Fire". The movies ______ made him famous, however, were the "Twilight"-movies. He played the role of Edward Cullen, a vampire ______ falls in love with the teenage girl Bella Swan.

	17				

						15		

This former child star is one of the first music stars ______ became famous via the Internet. The pop singer and songwriter ______ now lives in Hollywood, was born in Canada in 1994. His mum ______ always supported his interest in music, uploaded some videos on YouTube. Scooter Brown ______ works for a big record company, saw the videos and liked the young boy and his show.

		8			

		6			11

This American actor ______ has been described as one of the world's most attractive men, was born in 1963. He had already played in quite a lot of movies in the 1980s before he made movies like "Thelma & Louise", "Interview with the Vampire", "Seven", or "Fight Club" ______ made him really famous. Between 2001 and 2007 he played together with George Clooney ______ is one of his close friends, in the "Ocean's" series.

		1	3

		4	16

She was a blonde American actress, singer, model and showgirl ______ played in a number of successful movies in the 1950s. The real name of the actress, ______ was born in 1926, was Norma Jean Baker, but in the 1940s she took on a new name ______ made her famous. She played in films like "Some Like it Hot" or "How to Marry a Millionaire" ______ earned her a lot of fame. She was married three times and is said to have had an affair with John F. Kennedy ______ was American President at that time. She died in 1962 in her home in Los Angeles at the age of 36.

						2

	7				14

This American actress ______ was born in 1984, became a star when she was still very young. In 1994 at the age of nine she acted in the film "North" ______ was her first role ever. In 1998 she acted with Robert Redford in the film "The Horse Whisperer" which gained her a Young Star Award. She played girls or teenagers in a lot of other films before she switched to adult roles. In 2003 she acted the leading role in "Lost in Translation" ______ was the second big film by the director Sophia Coppola and was a big success for both – for the director and for the leading actress.

	9	10					

		5					13	

c) *Put the letters in the boxes. The little numbers help you with the right order. The solution sentence is one of the most popular sentences in Hollywood.*

1	2	3

4	5	6

7	8	9	10	11

12 G	13	14	15

16	17

d) *Make your own quiz about a famous star and let your partner guess who it is.*

Green Line 3/4
Vertretungsstunden
ISBN: 978-3-12-560036-2

Different people, different language

a) *What kind of language do you use with these people: casual, polite or very polite? Cut out the cards and put them in order from casual, to polite, to very polite.*

b) *Compare the results with your neighbour's. Do you have the same results? Where and why are your results different?*

casual — polite — very polite

your mother	your father	your best friend	your English teacher
your grandmother	a young shop assistant in a music shop	an old shop assistant in a shoe shop	a police officer
a student from school	a girl/boy you like very much	the waiter in a restaurant	your brother
your sister	your aunt	your uncle	your neighbour
a good friend of your parents	the mother of a friend	an old friend from primary school	an old woman you don't know

c) *There are different languages in different situations. Cut out these cards, too. Put them in one pile and the cards from exercise a) in another. Together with your partner, take one card from each pile (one person and one situation) and act out little dialogues.*

in a very expensive restaurant	at the bus stop	at school	at your parents' house
on the phone	in the supermarket	in a clothes store	at the post office
at the football stadium	at the airport	on an airplane	on vacation
in the swimming pool	on the bus	at the movies	at a party
in a computer store	at your grandmother's 80th birthday	on the street	at the ski-lift during vacation
in a fast food restaurant	at a newsagent's	in the park	???

Green Line 3/4
Vertretungsstunden
ISBN: 978-3-12-560036-2

1 Elements of a story

Match the elements with the right definition. Write the right number in the boxes.

1 setting | 2 genre | 3 plot | 4 character | 5 atmosphere | 6 narrator

The storyline or events which happen in a novel, film, drama, etc. ☐	A person in a drama, novel, film etc. There are main ones who are very important and less important ones. ☐	Category or kind of literature or film, e.g. comedy, tragedy, love story, western, etc. ☐
A person who tells a story. He/She tells it from his/her perspective and can be a character in the story. ☐	Describes the mood or tone of the story. It can be sad, scary, etc. – this is often done with the help of adjectives. ☐	The time and place when and where a drama, novel, film, etc. takes place, for example the story might be set in New York in the 1920s. ☐

2 Be the author – write the story

a) *Match the right elements. Which elements belong to which genres? Write down the right numbers.*

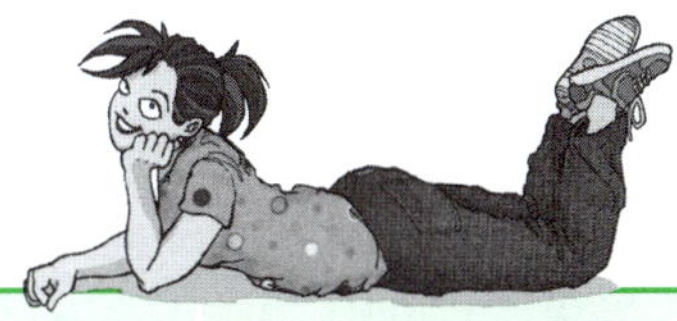

Genre	(1) Western	(2) Science Fiction	(3) Love Story	(4) Crime Story
Setting	**place:** planet Ulysses, **time:** in the year 2454 [2]	**place:** American high school in Phoenix, Arizona **time:** end of school year, 2013 ☐	**place:** Coxton, a small town in Nevada in the American West **time:** 1890s, hot summer ☐	**place:** Chicago, big city **time:** 1920s, foggy November ☐
Characters	**Amber**, 15 years old, a shy, clever student **Jacob**, 16 years old and very sporty **Amy**, 15 years old, very attractive but arrogant ☐	**Detective Wallace,** 63 years old, experienced detective **Warren Ellis**, 29 years old, his young and ambitious sergeant ☐	**John Walker**, good sheriff, wants to fight bandits[1] and villains[2] and protect[3] people **Gene McLain**, the villain, he robs people and is violent ☐	**Henoto**, the leader of the Hawks on planet Ulysses **Tyranto**, the leader of the Cheerios **Tiffylio**, the son of Tyranto, a strong fighter ☐
Plot	A dead body of a young man has been found near the Chicago River. Detective Wallace and Sergeant Ellis have arrived at the scene of crime. The dead body was the young lover of a rich old lady … ☐	The new sheriff John Walker arrives in the small town of Coxton. The villain Gene McLain isn't happy about that. He isn't seen for some days. But trains are robbed on their way to Coxton and one day McLain returns … ☐	People are running out of water on planet Ulysses; but they need water to survive, there is a war between the Hawks and the Cheerios about who has the power[4] over the water … ☐	Amber is secretly in love with Jacob. He likes her but doesn't know that she's in love with him. Amy has found out that Amber loves Jacob and wants to go out with him so that Amber won't get him … ☐

[1] **bandit** ['bændɪt] = Bandit • [2] **villain** ['vɪlən] = Schurke • [3] **protect** [prə'tekt] = (be)schützen • [4] **power** ['paʊə] = Macht

b) *Now choose one of the stories and write it.*

Green Line 3/4
Vertretungsstunden
ISBN: 978-3-12-560036-2

The Hollywood Sign

a) *Read the text and make a timeline about the history of the Hollywood Sign.*

The Hollywood Sign

The nine letters which make up the Hollywood Sign are probably the most famous letters in the world. They not only stand for the big film industry in Los Angeles; they are a symbol[1] of success, fame and stars.

Originally[2] the sign, which was first put up in 1923, had thirteen letters and it said "H-O-L-L-Y-W-O-O-D-L-A-N-D". It wasn't the film industry which built it. It was a real estate[3] company that wanted to advertise a new area for building houses in the Hollywood Hills. Each letter of the sign was 15 meters high and 9.1 meters wide. They were made of fabric[4], wood and metal and not meant to stay there forever, but only for the next 18 months. However, the American film industry became more and more famous in the 1920s and 30s and so did the sign.

Many people who came to Los Angeles dreamed of becoming a star, and the first thing they saw were the big letters in the Hollywood Hills.

In the 1940s the sign looked terrible: The letters were old, some were broken, and the "H" was completely missing. The sign now read "O-L-L-Y-W-O-O-D-L-A-N-D". In 1949 the film industry and the City of Los Angeles agreed to keep the sign and repair it. But they decided to take away the last four letters:

Now the sign read "H-O-L-L-Y-W-O-O-D". However, it didn't stay like that very long. After a few years the sign looked old and broken again, until in 1978 the rock musician Alice Cooper decided it was time for a new sign. Famous people and companies spent lots of money. Finally the old letters of fabric, wood and metal were taken down and new letters made of steel were put up.

They are still up in the Hollywood Hills today and can be seen from a great distance, especially after they were freshly painted in 2005.

b) *There is a debate[5]. Real estate companies want to sell the land on which the Hollywood Sign is built, take it down and build new houses. In groups of four, cut out the role cards and take one each. Find arguments for your position (the text above might help you) and start the debate.*

Role Card 1: Jason Hoover, 42 years, house owner

You and your family live in the neighborhood just above the Hollywood Sign. You are angry because tourists come to your neighborhood every day to get to the Hollywood Sign. You think that it would be better to take down the sign and to sell the land around it for new houses.

Role Card 2: Keira Daniels, 32 years, American actress

You have become a big star in Hollywood and your dream has come true. When you came to Hollywood the first thing you saw was the Hollywood Sign. You are shocked that people want to take it down because it has become the symbol of the American film industry.

Role Card 3: Cameron Simpson, 56 years, Mayor[6] of L.A.

You are shocked that people are thinking about taking down the Hollywood Sign; it's an important L.A. tourist attraction and the symbol of the American film industry. Many tourists come every year to see the sign. You are looking for people and companies to raise money to buy the area and keep the sign forever.

Role Card 4: Amanda Wright, 43 years, real estate company

Your real estate company put up the original Hollywoodland sign in 1923. You want to take it down, sell the land and build new houses there. The area is very expensive so you can make a lot of money with it. You don't think the sign is important because it was never *really* a sign for the film industry. Originally, it was a real estate company sign.

[1] **symbol** ['sɪmbl] = Symbol • [2] **originally** [ə'rɪdʒɪnəli] = ursprünglich • [3] **real estate** ['rɪəl ɪsteɪt] = Immobilien • [4] **fabric** ['fæbrɪk] = Stoff • [5] **debate** [dɪbeɪt] = Debatte • [6] **mayor** ['meə] = Bürgermeister

Green Line 3/4
Vertretungsstunden
ISBN: 978-3-12-560036-2

1 Famous athletes: A quiz

a) *Look at these athletes and match them with the right text. Write the correct number in the box.*

1. Usain Bolt | 2. Roger Federer | 3. Lionel Messi | 4. Serena Williams | 5. Dirk Nowitzki | 6. Michael Phelps | 7. Lindsey Vonn | 8. Sebastian Vettel

She's an American ski racer and has won 50 world cup races in her career. 7	He's an American swimmer and has won more than 15 Olympic gold medals. 6	He plays for FC Barcelona and is captain of the Argentina national team. 3	He plays for the Dallas Mavericks and he's 2.13 m tall. 5
He's from Jamaica and holds the world record in the 100- and 200-metre sprints. 1	She has won more than 26 Grand Slam titles and is a tennis player from America. 4	He's a tennis player and in 2008 he won 32 matches and didn't lose one! 2	He's a German Formula 1 racing driver and was world champion in 2010 and 2011. 8

b) *Now make sentences with relative clauses. Write them in your exercise book.*

Usain Bolt is the sprinter from Jamaica who holds the world record in the 100- and 200-metre sprints.

2 Tandem activity: A sports crossword puzzle

With a partner, take turns to explain your crossword puzzles to each other. Use relative clauses.

Example: It's a thing which you use … / It's a game which you can play with 11 people. / It's a person who can run …

Green Line 3/4 Vertretungsstunden ISBN: 978-3-12-560036-2

1 Working as a football reporter

a) *Read the speech bubbles. Who plays, who shoots the goals and who wins the match?*

b) *Put the speech bubbles in the right order. Write the numbers in the boxes.*

c) *What do the marked words mean? Explain them in English to your partner.*

d) *How would the reporter present the football commentary? Practise reading and try to make it as interesting as possible for the audience.*

1 Good evening. This is Peter Johnson, your **commentator**. Welcome to this match between Manchester United and Arsenal London, here at Etihad **Stadium** in Manchester.

7 Oh no, what's that? Miller is attacked by Brook. Foul! What is the referee going to do? He has seen it and blows his **whistle**. Yellow card for Brook and **penalty shot** for Arsenal.

2 The game starts. ManU's captain Manning **kicks off**.

8 Miller himself is going to do the penalty shot. ManU sets up a wall. Miller kicks the ball and it's a wonderful shot. O'Neil gets the ball; he's right in front of ManU's goal and scores. GOOOAAAL! It's the 63rd minute and that was the second goal of the match. A great goal by Tim O'Neil.

3 McAllister scores and … goal! Goooaaal!!!! Goal for Manchester. A beautiful goal by Rob McAllister in the 25th minute.

4 Forty-two minutes gone. The score is still one-nil but Arsenal has got the ball. Miller passes the ball to O'Neil, but O'Neil **misses** the ball. And now there's ManU's **defender** Brook who wins back the ball.

5 Welcome back for the second **half** of the match here at Etihad Stadium in Manchester. The score is one-nil and ManU was the better team in the first half of the game.

6 Arsenal seems to be stronger in this second half of the match. Sixty-two minutes gone. Arsenal's **midfielder** Podaya passes to Miller. Miller is now with the ball in front of ManU's goal. But here comes Brook …

9 And that's the referee's whistle. The game is over. One-one at the end of a beautiful match here at Etihad Stadium in Manchester.

2 Germany plays England: Write your own football report

a) *Have a look at the pictures and write your own football report.*

b) *How does the game end? Finish the football commentary.*

Green Line 3/4 Vertretungsstunden ISBN: 978-3-12-560036-2

Looking at … Football

A When did people start to play football? It's difficult to answer that question. There are a lot of old games in which people kicked some kind of ball. The old Greeks and Romans played a kind of football, but they were allowed to use their hands. So it was more like an early version of rugby! Similar games were played all over the world: in Australia, in New Zealand, but also in China and Japan.

B In the Middle Ages[1] football was already popular in England. Young men from two different villages often played against each other. There were two teams who had to get the ball into the goal of the other team. But the game was different from today: Each village had as many players as they wanted, there was no pitch, the play could last many hours, and there were no real rules. Often the whole match ended in a fight with broken noses! The king and the church didn't like this game and so they didn't allow people to play it. But a lot of young men still played the game.

C In the 18th and 19th century[2] football was very popular at English public schools. Again there were two teams, a ball, and two sticks in the ground were the goal. Many teachers weren't happy about the game because so many players got hurt. In 1828 a new headmaster[3], Thomas Arnold, came to the public school of Rugby. He thought sport was very important for the boys and football a good way to teach the boys how to play in a team. When the boys left school and went to university[4] they had a problem: The boys from other schools also played football but they had different rules. In 1848 students at Cambridge University wrote down the first football rules: Now there were goals, two teams with 15 to 20 players, shirts in different colours for the different teams, and only the goalkeeper[5] was allowed to use his hands with the ball.

D Football became more and more popular. The first football club was the FC Sheffield in the North of England in 1857. It is still there today. In 1862 players of different football clubs met in London and founded[6] the FA, the Football Association, and made new rules. Football wasn't popular only with English boys; boys in other parts of Europe started to play it, too. In 1874 the teacher Konrad Koch brought a football from England to his new school in Braunschweig and taught the boys how to play. They liked it, but not everyone in Germany was happy about that: Many felt that the boys should do athletics and not run after a ball!

E Today, people not only in Germany and England but almost everywhere in the world are crazy about football. In Germany more than 6 million people play football in 27,000 football clubs. Many are big fans and watch every game on TV or even go and watch their team play live. The players in the big football clubs make a lot of money. Football isn't just a game anymore – it has become a big business[7]!

[1] **Middle Ages** ['mɪdl‿eɪdʒɪz] = Mittelalter • [2] **century** ['sentʃri] = Jahrhundert • [3] **headmaster** ['hedmɑːstə] = Schulleiter/-in • [4] **university** [juːnɪ'vɜːsəti] = Universität • [5] **goalkeeper** ['gəʊlkiːpə] = Torwart • [6] **to found** [faʊnd] = gründen • [7] **business** ['bɪznɪs] = Geschäft

a) *Read the text and match the headlines with the paragraphs. Put the letters A–E into the boxes.*

Early ball games A | Football at public schools C | Football today E | Football fights in the Middle Ages B | Europe follows England's example D

b) *Summarize in one or two sentences what happened at different times in the history of football: BC (before Christ), in the Middle Ages, 18th and 19th century, in 1848, in 1857, in 1874, today.*

c) *Imagine you are a boy at an English public school in England in the 19th century. You write a letter to your friend back home and tell him about this new game – football – and how it is played.*

Start like this: Dear Thomas, I'm now at Eaton College in … At school we study hard but in our free time we often play a new game. It's called football and it's really fun. For football you need … *Go on.*

Green Line 3/4 Vertretungsstunden ISBN: 978-3-12-560036-2

A trip to a museum

a) *Class 9a went to the museum. Look at the speech bubbles and write down what they were and weren't allowed to do; what they had to do; and what they were and weren't able to do. Use your exercise book.*

b) *What do you know about Roman children? What were they able to do that you can't? What did they have to do that you don't have to do?*

c) *Kyle didn't go with the other children to the museum. Complete the gaps with the simple past or the past perfect and find out why not.*

Kyle wanted to leave the house when his mum saw that he hadn't cleaned (not; clean) his shoes. He was late but he had to (must) clean his shoes before he left the house. When Kyle arrived (arrive) at the bus stop his shoes were clean, but the bus had already gone (already; go). He ran (run) to school, but when he got (get) there his class had already left (already; leave) on the school bus. He had to stay at school. When it was (be) time to go home, Kyle hadn't learned (not; learn) very much about the Romans, but his shoes were still clean.

d) *Look at the picture of Class 9a. Here they are on their way home from the museum. Look at their faces/actions. What do you think had happened earlier at the museum? Write a short text. Be creative!*

Green Line 3/4 Vertretungsstunden ISBN: 978-3-12-560036-2

Looking at … A famous person in history

Read these texts and answer the questions below.

The lady with the lamp

"Oh, I love James. He's so funny and kind. I want to marry him! I hope he asks me," said Frances. "Why don't you ask him?" asked Florence, smiling. "Oh, don't be silly. I can't ask a man to marry me. Women aren't allowed to do that. Women have to look nice, play the piano and paint! And a lady has to wait for a man to marry her. Oh, I wish I was a man. Or I wish I was beautiful like you and then I could choose anybody I wanted."

"Well, I'm not going to marry a man. I'm going to become a nurse and work in a hospital," replied Florence.

Frances laughed at first – women don't work – but then saw that Florence wasn't smiling.

Dear Frances,

It's quarter past one in the morning and I can't sleep. Klara has just died and I feel so sad, I just want to cry. She had six children and the youngest is only two weeks old. How will they survive without their mother? I want to look after them but I can't. Sometimes I'd just like to go home and forget all this. It's too much. It's too hard. Why does God[1] do this to people? But then I talk to Theodor Fliedner and I can see how we can improve things. He's such a good teacher and he's so kind and gentle. We have to teach people how to stay clean; to wash their hands when they have touched somebody who is ill; and to drink clean water. When I qualify as a nurse, I will leave Germany and go back to London and look after people there.

Is Mum still angry with me? I didn't want to hurt her, but I just had to come here and learn to become a nurse. God wanted it this way …

Dear Jenny,

Things have improved here. Some nurses have arrived and they can now look after us better so that not as many soldiers die every day. Florence Nightingale comes around every night with a lamp and looks after us. She gives us something to drink and talks to us. The pain is never as bad when she's there. My dearest Jenny, I, too, will survive but I have to prepare you for a shock. I now only have one leg. But the important thing is that I still love you. I know that life will not be so easy now. It will be more difficult to work and to live. If you never want to see me again, I will understand.

Your ever-loving Henry

[1] **God** [gɒd] = Gott

a) *Are these sentences true or false?*

	true	false
1. This story possibly happened in the last fifty years.		✔
2. Florence wanted to get married quickly.		✔
3. Florence believed in God.	✔	
4. Florence learnt how to become a nurse in London.		✔
5. Florence Nightingale was 'the lady with the lamp'.	✔	
6. Henry lost both his legs in the war.		✔

b) *What do these words mean in the text? Tick the right answers.*

1. lamp (line 39)	☐ Tablette	☑ Licht	☐ Messer
2. nurse (line 11)	☐ Pfarrerin	☐ Lehrerin	☑ Krankenschwester
3. qualify (line 29)	☑ berechtigt werden	☐ lernen	☐ unterrichten

c) *Write a short description of Florence Nightingale's life. What do you know about her?*

Think about: • her family • the places she went to • her life • her character

d) *Write a short description of the other characters: Frances, Theodor and Henry. What do you think they are like? What happens to them? Who else do they know?*

Green Line 3/4
Vertretungsstunden
ISBN: 978-3-12-560036-2

Tandem activity: Stratford-upon-Avon

Partner A

You have information about two places that you can visit in Stratford. Answer your partner's questions about them. Your partner has information about two **other** *places in Stratford. Ask your partner about them and complete the information.*

Boating on the Avon	**Royal Shakespeare Company Theatre**
The Avon is a beautiful river which goes through the centre of Stratford and past the biggest theatre in town. You can go on boats here from spring to autumn and row up and down the river. There's no better way to see Stratford. Prices: 1 rowing boat: £7.50 per hour	There are three theatres in this building, so you can be sure you'll find something that you like. You'll be able to choose between Shakespeare's plays and more modern ones. You can also do courses at the theatre, or go on a tour there. The theatre is in the centre of town, near the river. Tickets: from £20 Children: £12.50
Shakespeare's Birthplace	**Anne Hathaway's Cottage**
What can you do/see there? *go on a tour of the house, find out how he lived*	What can you do/see there? *find out about Shakespeare's plays, look around the house*
How much does it cost? *£ 12.50 adults, £ 7.50 children*	How much does it cost? *£ 7.50 adults, £ 4.50 children*
Where is it? *in the centre of town*	Where is it? *a mile away from Stratford*

Partner B

You have information about two places that you can visit in Stratford. Answer your partner's questions about them. Your partner has information about two **other** *places in Stratford. Ask your partner about them and complete the information.*

Shakespeare's Birthplace	**Anne Hathaway's Cottage**
William Shakespeare was born in this house in 1564. This is also where he lived with his wife Anne Hathaway for the first five years. You can go on tours of the house and find out about his life and how he lived here. It is in the centre of town. Prices: Adults: £12.50 Children: £7.50 Shakespeare Pass (3 Shakespeare houses in a day): Adults: £19 Children: £10	This is the place where Shakespeare's wife lived before she married him. It is a mile away from Stratford. You can look around the house and feel what life was like at the time. In the beautiful garden you can find out more about Shakespeare's plays. Prices: Adults: £7.50 Children: £4.50
Boating on the Avon	**Royal Shakespeare Company Theatre**
What can you do/see there? *Stratford and the theatre, go rowing*	What can you do/see there? *watch Shakespeare's plays or modern ones, do courses*
How much does it cost? *£ 7.50 per hour*	How much does it cost? *from £ 20, £ 12.50 children*
Where is it? *in the centre of Stratford*	Where is it? *centre of town near the river*

Green Line 3/4
Vertretungsstunden
ISBN: 978-3-12-560036-2

1 All about Michelle

a) *Complete the gaps with the correct reflexive pronoun, 'each other' nothing (–).*

Michelle is now six years old and she has changed *–* a lot. She can look after *herself*. She's very clean and she washes *herself* a lot. She can feed *herself*, too, but mum usually feeds her. My brother is nine years old and he and Michelle often play with *each other*. They usually enjoy *themselves* but my brother isn't always nice to her. Michelle can even go out alone. She and her friends often meet *each other / –* in our garden but sometimes they fight and hurt *each other*. Then my mum runs out and shouts, "Can't you behave *yourselves / –*?" Michelle never gets *–* lost, and when she comes in, she sits *–* down on the sofa and relaxes *–*. We all love Michelle and although she's just a cat, she's still part of the family.

b) *Write down everything you did today in German. Then write it in English. Underline all the reflexive verbs in the German and in the English texts.*

Meine Mutter hat mich um 6:30 geweckt und dann …

2 The Patterson family

a) *Read the play "Home alone" again and complete the sentences.*

1. If Grandpa was able to look after himself, he *wouldn't need to leave* his home.
2. If the cleaning lady hadn't told Terry and Sally about Grandpa's problem, they *wouldn't have visited* him.
3. Mel and Amy won't be able to have their own rooms if Grandpa *moves into the house*.
4. They would probably have had more fun at the party if their parents *hadn't come home* again.

b) *Partner work! Write some questions for your partner.*
Start like this:

What would you have done if …?
What will you do if …?
What would you do if …?

c) *Now answer your partner's questions.*

Green Line 3/4
Vertretungsstunden
ISBN: 978-3-12-560036-2

An argument

Read the story and answer the questions.

"Look at him. Isn't he good-looking?" Jeanie asked. "Yes, he is," said Ella, "but I don't think he likes me." Jeanie was showing Ella photos of her and her new boyfriend. Ella felt a bit jealous, of course. Jeanie often went out with Harvey now, and not with her.

"He likes you, but he's a bit jealous," Jeanie answered, "because you're my best friend."

"If I had a boyfriend, we could all go out together," said Ella. "Saturdays are usually a bit boring now. Nobody wants to go out with me."

"I know. Let's go out this Saturday. I'm going for a hike with my parents in the afternoon, but I'll call you when I get back. We could go to the cinema," suggested Jeanie.

On Saturday evening Ella waited for Jeanie to call. She waited and waited but Jeanie didn't call. Ella got angrier and angrier. "What kind of friend is that? She's probably gone out with Harvey and forgotten me," she thought. When the phone rang, she was so angry that she almost didn't answer it. When she answered it, it wasn't Jeanie, it was Jack. "Do you want to come to the cinema with me?" asked Jack. "I've got two tickets but my friend Henry's ill and can't come."

Two hours later Ella and Jack went to the cinema together. They also saw Jeanie and Harvey there.

At school on Monday Ella heard Jeanie tell a friend that she'd had a great day on Saturday.

"I'm glad that you had a good day, Jeanie. I'm sure it would have been boring if you'd gone out with me."

"What's your problem? First you tell me that I never go out with you and then you can't even wait for me to call you!" replied Jeanie. "When I called you, your parents said that you'd already gone out."

"I waited until 6 pm but you didn't call. I knew you *really* wanted to go out with Harvey. Boyfriends are more important than best friends, of course," said Ella angrily.

"Oh, you always talk badly about Harvey. Just because *you* haven't got a boyfriend! Or you *didn't* have a boyfriend. But as soon as a boy asks you, you forget about me, don't you?" shouted Jeanie.

"Oh, that's just so unfair! And I thought you were my best friend. Well, not now!" shouted Ella back and walked away.

a) *Answer the questions below with words or phrases.*

1. How did Ella feel about Harvey? *jealous*
2. What did Jeanie do on Saturday? *went for a hike, went to the cinema*
3. Why did Ella feel angry on Saturday? *Because Jeanie didn't call.*
4. Who did Ella go to the cinema with? *Jack*
5. Why didn't Jack go with Henry? *Henry was ill.*
6. Did Jeanie call Ella? *Yes, she did.*

b) *What did Jeanie and Ella do wrong when they were fighting on Monday?*

Jeanie	Ella
She didn't stay cool. She said "You always talk badly about Harvey."	*She got angry and walked away. She didn't stay cool.*

c) *Write the conversation again. This time, the girls should both stay friendly.*

Green Line 3/4
Vertretungsstunden
ISBN: 978-3-12-560036-2

1 Tandem activity: Telephone messages

Read the notes and act out the telephone messages. First act out message 1. Partner A answers the phone and Partner B leaves the message. Partner A writes down the message and Partner B checks it. Then take turns for message 2.

Partner A Message 1	Partner A Message 2
Melde dich. (Hello, this is … Is Ellen there?)	(Hello?) *Sag, dass du gern mit Chris sprechen möchtest.*
Sag, dass Ellen noch in der Schule ist. Frage, ob du ihr etwas ausrichten kannst. (Yes, please. I'm having a party at my house. Ellen can come over around 7 o'clock.)	(I'm afraid he isn't at home now. Can I take a message?) *Sage, dass er dich vor 19.30 zurückrufen soll.*
Frage nach dem Namen und der Adresse des Anrufers. (My name's Bailey and I live in 15, Barton Road.)	(I'll tell him. What's your name and does Chris have your telephone number?) *Du heißt Abigail und deine Telefonnummer ist 0162 549 3425.*

Partner B Message 1	Partner B Message 2
(Hello?) *Sag hallo und frage, ob Ellen da ist.*	*Melde dich.* (Hello, this is … I'd like to speak to Chris, please.)
(Ellen is still at school. Can I take a message?) *Sag, dass du eine Party gibst und Ellen einladen möchtest. Sie kann ab 19.00 vorbeikommen.*	*Sage, dass er nicht da ist und frage, ob du etwas ausrichten sollst.* (Could he call me back before 7.30, please?)
(What's your name and where do you live?) *Sage, dass du Bailey heißt und in der Barton Road 15 wohnst.*	*Frage, wie der Anrufer heißt und ob Chris die Telefonnummer hat.* (My name is Abigail and my phone number is 0162 549 3425.)

2 A play: Messages gone wrong!

a) *Read the short story and complete the grid about the messages.*

Corey calls his parents after school to say that he is going to his friend Taylor's house to do some homework. His parents aren't there and he leaves a message on the answering machine. He's actually going to a party at Ashley's house. Corey calls his friend, Taylor, to tell him what to say if his parents call. Taylor isn't there. Corey leaves a message with his parents to tell Taylor to call him back on his mobile. Taylor gets home and tries to call Corey, but Corey doesn't hear his mobile because it's in his bag. Ashley hears it and answers it. Taylor tells Ashley he wants to speak to Corey and Ashley invites him to the party, too.

Call	Who called?	Who did they speak to?	Who did they want to speak to?	What was the message about?
1	Corey	answerphone	*his parents*	*Corey going to Taylor's house*
2	*Corey*	*Taylor's parents*	*Taylor*	*Taylor should call him back.*
3	*Taylor*	*Ashley*	*Corey*	*He wanted to speak to Corey, Ashley invited him.*

b) *In groups, decide how the story ends. Write the story as a play and act it out for your class. Decide who is going to be Corey, Taylor, Ashley, Taylor's mum or dad, and Corey's mum or dad.*

Green Line 3/4
Vertretungsstunden
ISBN: 978-3-12-560036-2

1 How to help people / Asking for help

Have a look at the following phrases. Underline phrases you can use if you want to help people in green and phrases you can use if you need help in black.

Excuse me, can you …	That's no problem.	I'm sorry, but …
Thank you very much.	That's very kind of you.	Don't worry. I can help you.
Could you … for me?	Never mind.	You've been a great help.
You're welcome.	That's OK.	Can you do me a favour?

2 Tandem activity: How to help people

a) *Cut out these situation cards. Each partner gets one card. Write little dialogues for the situations.*

Situation 1, Partner A
You're Chris, you're 14 years old and you're on your way to school. At the bus station you see an old lady. She looks lost. You ask her if you can help her.

Situation 2, Partner A
You're Kristen, you're 35 years old and you have got a little son, Jason (1 year). You have to go to work in an hour. Now the baby sitter just called and told you that she's ill and can't come. You can't take Jason with you. You go to your neighbour, Miranda, and want to ask her for help. Her daughter Keira, 14, opens the door.

Situation 3, Partner A
You're Steven, you're 15 years old. You met Jasmine at a party and you really liked her. But Jasmine doesn't go to your school and you don't have her telephone number. You ask your friend Mike for help.

Situation 1, Partner B
You're Maureen, you're 77 years old and you want to visit your son who lives in a different city. You arrived by train and now you need to take a bus, but you've forgotten which one. You just know that you need to get off at Lancaster Street.

Situation 2, Partner B
You're Keira, you're 14 years old. You love little children and do babysitting in your free time. You live with your mother, Miranda, in a flat, but your mother isn't at home. Suddenly the doorbell rings. It's Kristen, the neighbour from next door with her little son, Jason. You like Jason very much and want to help her.

Situation 3, Partner B
You're Mike, you're 15 years old and your friend is Steven. You went to a party with him two weeks ago. Steven talked to a girl at the party, Jasmine. You know her because she's a friend of your sister. Now Steven has a problem. Can you help him?

b) *Now choose one scene and act it out to your class.*

3 A new pupil

Simon is a new pupil in Rhona and Shirin's class. He has moved with his family from York to Swansea.

a) *Everything is new for Simon: a new house, a new city, a new school, a new class … and he doesn't know anyone. How does he feel before he goes to his new school for the first time?*

b) *Shirin can understand how Simon feels because she was new in Swansea a year ago. She's thinking about what she and her class could do to make Simon feel welcome. Now think about it yourself and write down at least four of five ideas.*

c) *Decide on one idea and write a dialogue between Shirin, Rhona and Simon.*

Green Line 3/4
Vertretungsstunden
ISBN: 978-3-12-560036-2

1 Reading factual texts

Snowdonia National Park in the North of Wales has a great landscape with beautiful mountains. Every year thousands of tourists come here to go hiking and especially to climb Mount Snowdon, the highest mountain in England and Wales. On top of Mount Snowdon you have a great view over Snowdonia National Park. But every year tourists get into trouble because they don't follow important safety rules. There were more than 400 calls for help from hikers and climbers last year on Wales' biggest mountain. For two people the help came too late, and they died.

It's important to plan a Mount Snowdon tour carefully. Tourists should watch the weather forecasts. But keep in mind that temperatures up on the mountain are usually colder than down in the valley[1], and the weather in the mountains can change very quickly. So it's important to take warm clothes like trousers, a hat and a good jacket[2]. It's not a good idea to wear jeans – they dry very slowly. And don't forget good hiking boots! You should also bring some extra food and drink. It's not enough to buy a map and a compass – you also must know how to use them. You should also bring a mobile phone to call for help, but it's even more important that you let people know where you're going. It's a good idea to bring a whistle[3] and a torch[4]; in case of emergency you can make signals and show rescue[5] teams where you are. If you need any advice on mountain safety call the Mountain Rescue at 01690 720333.

[1]valley [ˈvæli] = Tal • [2]jacket [ˈdʒækɪt] = Jacke • [3]whistle [ˈwɪsl] = Pfeife • [4]torch [tɔːtʃ] = Taschenlampe, Fackel • [5]rescue [ˈreskjuː] = Rettung

a) *Skim the text. What is it about?*

b) *Where can you find information like this? Tick the right answers.*

- ✔ in a travel guide
- ☐ in a dictionary
- ☐ in a sports magazine
- ☐ in a brochure for outdoor equipment
- ✔ on the website of the Mountain Rescue team

c) *Write down important mountain safety rules. Use imperative forms.*
Example: Watch the weather forecast before you go.

2 Rhona's adventure in the mountains

This year Rhona's family are spending their holidays in Snowdonia National Park in the North of Wales. This is an e-mail she writes to her friend Shirin.

Dear Shirin,
Dad wanted to get to know the "real Wales" so this year we're spending our holidays in Snowdonia National Park. We're staying at Pen y Pass youth hostel which is close to Mount Snowdon, the highest mountain in England and Wales. Yesterday we wanted to climb it. We started early in the morning. The weather was great so we could just wear jeans and a T-shirt and didn't have to take any jackets. The first part was long but OK. After about two hours mum said: "Shall we go to this lake? It looks so beautiful." But dad said: "No, let's go on. We want to get to the top. This way." So we went on. After a while the path got more dangerous and it was getting really difficult to climb. And mum was getting really angry! Dad said that we must have taken the wrong path and he didn't have a map. We had also forgotten to take our mobiles! But dad said: "Don't worry. When we're at the top there'll be a restaurant and an easy way down. We can even go down on the Snowdon Mountain Railway. Doesn't that sound good?" So we went on. The last part was quite dangerous. There was no path at all and we were wearing only trainers! And it was getting really cold and foggy. When we finally arrived at the top, a big surprise was waiting for us. There was no restaurant, no railway and also no easy way down! It wasn't Mount Snowdon but Crib Goch. We had climbed the wrong mountain!

a) *Which mountain safety rules did Rhona and her family **not** follow?*

b) *How does Rhona's adventure go on? Write an ending to the story.*

Green Line 3/4
Vertretungsstunden
ISBN: 978-3-12-560036-2

Who wants to be a 'Britonaire'?

People in Great Britain are crazy about quizzes. A lot of people go to pub quizzes or table quizzes and play in groups of 4–5. Each team sits at one table and works together. The team with the most correct answers wins. Play this table quiz about Britain in your class.

I Geography (the map in the book might help you)

1. What is the capital of Northern Ireland?
   B E L F A S T
2. Which river runs through Newcastle?
   T Y N E
3. What is the name of the highest mountain in Wales?
   S N O W D O N
4. What is the biggest English island?
   I S L E O F M A N

II Famous Britons

Have a look at these faces and write down the name of these famous British people.

The Queen

Shakespeare

Charlie Chaplin

Robin Hood

III Britain in numbers

1. How many people live in the UK?
   a) about 122 million b) about 62 million ✔ c) about 202 million d) about 92 million
2. How many people fit into Wembley Stadium, London?
   a) 90,000 ✔ b) 20,000 c) 1,000,000 d) 5,000
3. How long is the channel tunnel between England and France?
   a) 100,5 km b) 10,5 km c) 50,5 km ✔ d) 5,5 km
4. How many kilometres are one mile?
   a) about 1.609 km ✔ b) about 0.604 km c) about 2.807 km d) about 0.100 km

IV Records

1. Who had six wives?
   a) David Beckham b) King Henry VIII ✔ c) Prince Charles d) John Lennon
2. The village with the longest name is *Llanfairpwllgwyngyllgogerychwyrndrobwll-llantysiliogogogoch*. Where can you find it?
   a) in Scotland b) in England c) in Wales ✔ d) in Northern Ireland
3. How high is Ben Nevis, the highest mountain in the UK?
   a) 2,422 metres b) 1,815 metres c) 887 metres d) 1,343 metres ✔
4. What is the name of Scotland's biggest pet?
   a) Josie b) Nessie ✔ c) Rosie d) Lindsay

V Famous Places

Have a look at these places and write down the name.

Windsor Castle

Tower Bridge

Albert Dock

Millennium Centre

VI Facts

1. What is the name of the British flag?
   U N I O N J A C K
2. The national anthem of Great Britain is called:
   God Save the *Q U E E N*
3. What is the name of a famous pop band from Liverpool?
   T H E B E A T L E S
4. People in Germany pay in euros, people in Britain in …
   P O U N D S

Green Line 3/4
Vertretungsstunden
ISBN: 978-3-12-560036-2

Looking at … Soaps in Britain

a) *Read about two soaps which are shown regularly in Britain: EastEnders and Neighbours. Match the paragraphs to the right soap and put them in the right order.*

A This soap opera is about people who live in the East End of London. It is filmed by the BBC in their studios in North London. It's shown on the BBC four times a week. It was first shown on British TV on 19th February 1985 and it became very popular very quickly. It is still one of the BBC's most popular programmes. The soap is also shown in many countries around the world, for example the USA and Australia.

B This soap is written mostly for younger people and so it's shown at 6:30 pm. Problems with school and parents are shown and also more serious[1] problems, e.g. with the police or with health. But the soap never stays too serious for long. When the problems become too much, the characters can always get away to the beach. For the makers of the soap the biggest problem is where the soap will go in the future. Will it win the competition with other Australian soaps?

C In 2010 this soap opera was the most popular on British television but it's also the soap opera that creates the most problems for the BBC. It's shown at 7:30 or 8:00 pm in the evening – when young people are watching – but the characters use language and have problems which many people say should *not* be shown to younger people. The BBC have no plans to change anything in the future.

D London's East End is one of the poorer parts of the city, and this can clearly be seen in the soap. The characters in the soap live in small houses or flats and often have money problems. Everything usually happens in their houses, shops and at the pub. The writers of the soap wanted it to show real life and so it often shows real-life problems. One teenage girl had a baby at 15 and some characters have had to go to prison or even die.

E This is an Australian soap opera which was first shown in Australia on 18th March 1985. It is filmed by the Australian company "Ten" in a real street in Melbourne, but it's also sometimes filmed in different parts of Australia and around the world. It was shown in Britain for the first time in 1986 and is now more popular in Britain than in Australia. At first it was shown on BBC One but it is now shown by Channel 5.

F The characters in this soap opera live or work in a part of the city which is definitely not poor. You see the characters in their houses, schools or cafés. Also a lot of the action is outside – in gardens or even on the beach. The writers of the soap wanted to show how young people deal with older people; many young actors have begun their careers in this series. Kylie Minogue, for example, first became famous in this soap.

[1] **serious** ['sɪərɪəs] = ernst

EastEnders: Paragraphs *A, D, C* Neighbours: Paragraphs *E, F, B*

b) *Complete the grid about the two soap operas.*

	EastEnders	Neighbours
Where is it made?	*in the BBC studios in North London*	*in a real street in Melbourne*
Who makes it?	*BBC*	*Ten*
Where is it shown?	*many countries (UK, USA, Australia …)*	*Britain and Australia*
Storyline	*real-life problems for families in the east of London*	*problems with school and parents, young and old people*

c) *Find out about a German soap opera and write about it in your exercise book.*

Green Line 3/4
Vertretungsstunden
ISBN: 978-3-12-560036-2

1 Media and more!

a) *Complete the gaps in the two short texts with the correct form of the verb. Use the simple present form of the passive. Then draw lines to match the texts to the things they describe.*

1. It *is written* (write) by many authors who *aren't paid* (not; pay). Every day it *is used* (use) by millions of people all over the world. In this way information *is shared* (share) by people who can use the Internet.
2. These *are shown* (show) every day on most TV channels. They *are often done* (often; do) very cleverly and are fun to watch. It *is hoped* (hope) that people will buy the things which *are shown* (show).

The Internet · Ebay · Wikipedia · The Radio · Soaps · Advertisements

b) *Write texts using the passive to describe the other things in 1a). You can also describe other media words. Give your texts to a partner. Can your partner guess what they describe?*

2 Media!

Rewrite the text about computers with the passive. Be careful: Not every sentence can be written in the passive! Use your exercise book. Start like this: The media are used for …

People use the media for information and communication. People know that the Romans used a kind of newspaper thousands of years ago. Men wrote out information in the market place in Rome. Romans read about great battles which Julius Caesar had won. Hundreds of years later they made newspapers and books out of paper.
Plays were also an early form of media. People performed plays in towns all over the world. People watched them for entertainment but also for information. With the invention of television and radio, a much larger audience could get entertainment and information. These new media also informed people more quickly about what happened in other parts of the world.
In the last fifty years modern technology has greatly improved communication. The modern media have changed our whole life. How will new inventions change it in the future?

3 A party for the stars!

a) *Look at the sentences below. Tick the ones in which the verbs have two objects.*

1. ☑ A rich actor sent an invitation to many important directors and actors.
2. ☑ He made wonderful food for his guests.
3. ☐ Some famous pop stars played great music at his party.
4. ☑ At the end of the evening a director offered the rich actor a great role in a new film.
5. ☐ The actor has organised many other parties since then.
6. ☑ In the last few years other directors have promised him good roles.

b) *Rewrite the sentences which you ticked in a) in both forms of the passive (Passive 1 and Passive 2) in your exercise book. Underline the passive form which you think would sound better in a text.*

Green Line 3/4
Vertretungsstunden
ISBN: 978-3-12-560036-2

1 Book Quiz: The media

What do you remember about the media? Choose the right answer to the questions below. Then check your answers in the book.

1. When was the first colour TV made?	☐ 1914	☐ 1934	☑ 1954	☐ 1974
2. When did the BBC start?	☐ 1902	☑ 1922	☐ 1942	☐ 1962
3. What was the first Internet search engine called?	☑ Lycos	☐ Google	☐ Yahoo	☐ Alltheweb
4. When did the Times newspaper start?	☐ 1685	☐ 1735	☑ 1785	☐ 1835
5. Which of these are "popular" newspapers?	☐ The Times		☑ The Sun	
	☐ The Telegraph		☑ The Daily Mirror	
6. Who created the first browser?	☑ Tim Berners-Lee		☐ Bill Gates	
	☐ Steve Jobs		☐ Steve Wozniak	
7. When did the World Wide Web start?	☐ 1961	☐ 1971	☐ 1981	☑ 1991
8. Which British soap has been on TV the longest?	☐ EastEnders		☑ Coronation Street	
	☐ Neighbours		☐ Emmerdale Farm	

2 General knowledge: The Internet!

a) *Can you guess the right numbers? Use the Internet to check your answers.*

1. How many friends does a Facebook user have on average?
2. How many Twitter accounts are there?
3. How many videos are watched on YouTube every day?
4. How many years would you need to live to watch *all* the videos on YouTube?
5. How many articles are there in Wikipedia?
6. How many people use Facebook regularly?
7. How many minutes do people spend on Facebook each visit?
8. What per cent of Internet users read blogs[1]?

b) *Now research the Internet habits[2] of your class. Write questions and give them to the pupils in your class to answer. Examples:*

Do you use Facebook? How often do you download music?

c) *Put the results you got in b) in a grid and present them to your class.*

[1] **blog** [blɒg] = Blog; Internettagebuch • [2] **habit** ['hæbɪt] = Gewohnheit

Green Line 3/4
Vertretungsstunden
ISBN: 978-3-12-560036-2

1 On holiday on the Isle of Wight

a) *Match the questions and answers (or comments and replies). Draw lines.*

1. Glen: How long are you staying on the island?
2. Sally: Have you ever been here before?
3. Glen: Where did you go yesterday?
4. Glen: What will the weather be like tomorrow?
5. Glen: Can you go surfing on this island?
6. Sally: Would you like to go surfing with us tomorrow?

- Glen: Yes, I came here two years ago.
- Sally: Yes, but go to the island west of the island if you want to go surfing; the waves are better there.
- Sally: We're staying till next Saturday.
- Sally: We went to Steephill Cove.
- Glen: That'd be great, but I can't surf.
- Sally: It will be windy but cold.

b) *Now report the short dialogues from a) in indirect speech. Write them in your exercise book.*

Glen asked how long Sally was staying …

2 Report a dialogue

Partner work: Choose (part of) a dialogue from the book and report it. Give it to your partner. He/she should give you his/her reported dialogue at the same time. Who can find the original dialogue in the book first?

TIP
Report about 6 lines of dialogue – but don't make it too difficult for your partner!

3 An indirect speech game

Play this game in groups of three or four.

1. Split into groups of three or four.
2. Everybody writes four sentences (questions, statements and commands) on different pieces of paper and reports the sentences on the back of the paper.
3. The groups exchange their sentences.
4. Put the sentences on the table between the group.
5. The first person reads a sentence.
6. The second person should report it.
   If the person reports the sentence correctly, they get the piece of paper and can read the next sentence.
   If they report the sentence incorrectly, the next person can try.
7. The winner is the person who can get the most pieces of paper.

Green Line 3/4
Vertretungsstunden
ISBN: 978-3-12-560036-2

Looking at … Transport in Britain

a) *Match the texts below to the types of transport they describe.*

Train travel: C Coach travel: D London Transport: A Greater Manchester Transport: B

A I don't know which website you were looking at but no, you don't need to get a travelcard before you come. The best thing is to get an Oyster card when you get them from the station or from newsagents. They cost 5 pounds but you get that back when you give the Oyster card back at the end of your holiday. They're great. You can put some money on your card (like a top-up card for your mobile) and then every time you use it – on the bus or the Tube – the money is taken from your card. It's so much easier than buying a ticket every time you travel! And it's a lot cheaper, too. You can even use them for boat transport on the Thames. If you want to I could buy one for you before you come. What do you think?

B
AP91: I've just sold my car and I can't work out how the transport system works. Can anyone out there help me?
Peggy7: Just look on the website: tfgm.com and you can find out everything.
Busfan123: In the centre of Manchester you can catch the No. 1 and the No. 2 buses and they're free.
Oldlady: If you're over 60, you can travel free.
EricA40: The Metrolink is great but remember to buy your ticket before you get on the tram!
AP91: There's no Metrolink near me. What about buses?
Busfan123: It's cheapest if you get a return ticket, but you must use the same company[1] for both ways.

C Went to Brighton today. Fantastic. Met Rachel and went to the beach. It only took an hour and it wasn't too expensive because I bought a day return ticket (£22.50). Then I wanted to go home. And that's when the problems started! I'd promised mum I'd be home at 8 pm. Test at school tomorrow! So I wanted to get the train at 6:17 pm but I missed it. No problem – I thought. But I couldn't get the next train at 6:34 – it was a different train company which I couldn't use with my ticket! I couldn't believe it. I didn't know you had to get different tickets for different companies! I was NOT happy – the man in the ticket office said you can get tickets for all the trains but they're more expensive! So I was late, mum was angry, and now I'm worried about the test tomorrow. Stupid trains!

D
Cheapest fares Manchester to London!
Journey time from 4 hours 30 minutes.
Check out our services to airports.
All coaches have toilets!

[1]company ['kʌmpəni] = Unternehmen

b) *Match the texts to the types of text below.*

Advertisement: D Diary entry: C E-mail: A Internet chat: B

c) *Read the statements about the texts and decide if they are true or false.*

	true	false
1. If you buy an Oyster card, you can travel all around London for £5.		✔
2. There are different train companies in England.	✔	
3. The Metrolink is a bus company in Manchester.		✔
4. People pay different fares on the coach – it's only cheap if you buy early.	✔	

d) *Rewrite text B as an advertisement. Rewrite text C as an e-mail.*

A look at the map in the front of your book and Kelsey's web album will help you to answer these quizzes.

1 Tandem activity: The 50 states of the US

Give these clues to a partner. He/She has to find out the right state and find it on the map.

Partner A

Give Partner B these clues.

1. It's next to Mexico and home to the Grand Canyon.
2. Its capital Detroit is famous for its car industry.
3. This state is next to Canada. It's very big and cold here.
4. Many tourists visit this US state with its warm weather and its long coast. In its national parks you can even find alligators.
5. New Orleans is the capital of this state which is famous for its jazz music.
6. The Statue of Liberty "lives" in this state.
7. This state is in the South, next to North Carolina and Georgia.
8. This is the youngest of the United States. It's made up of islands and it's in the middle of the Pacific Ocean.

Partner B

Give Partner A these clues.

1. The battle of Wounded Knee took place here.
2. You can find the White House, the home of the US president, here.
3. This is the second biggest US state and it's on the Mexican border[1].
4. Route 66 starts in San Francisco and ends in this state.
5. In this state you can find Hollywood – the centre of the film industry.
6. Yellowstone National Park can be found in this state.
7. This is the biggest state in New England.
8. This state has the same name as its most important city. You can find it on the East Coast.

[1]border ['bɔːdə] = Grenze

2 A crossword puzzle

a) *Look at the clues and fill in the crossword puzzle.*

Across
4. highest mountain in the US
5. This part of the US is called the Corn Belt.
6. This ocean can be found on the East Coast of America.
7. a famous national park
8. mountains which go through the states of Wyoming, Colorado and New Mexico

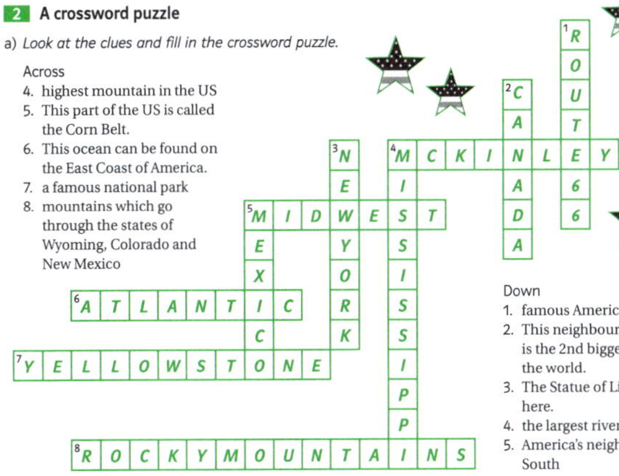

Down
1. famous American highway
2. This neighbour north of the US is the 2nd biggest country in the world.
3. The Statue of Liberty "lives" here.
4. the largest river in the US
5. America's neighbour to the South

b) *Create your own USA crossword puzzle and give it to a partner.*

Looking at … The Statue of Liberty

a) *The Statue of Liberty has many symbols[1]. Look at the pictures, the words and the texts and match them. Use a dictionary if you need help.*

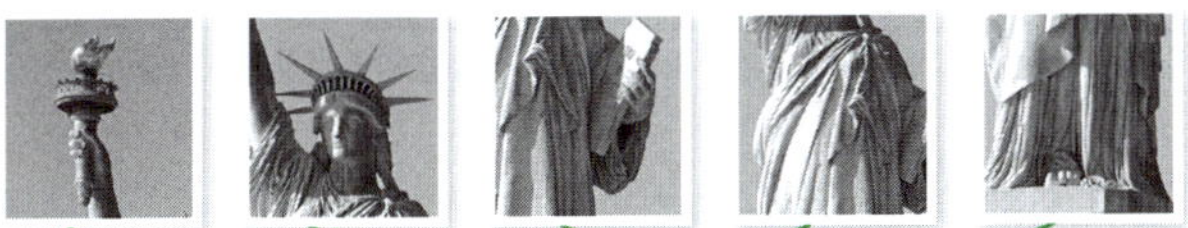

robe · crown · torch · broken chains · law book

a) Prisoners used to have chains around their feet. But these chains are broken. She's free.

b) The statue holds this in her right hand. The light is a symbol of hope.

c) This looks like a dress of the Roman goddess Libertas – which means 'liberty'.

d) This book is the Constitution of the US – the rights of the people.

e) The seven spikes look like the sun (= light) and stand for the seven seas and continents.

[1]symbol ['sɪmbl] = Symbol

b) *Put the following paragraphs about the history of the Statue of Liberty in the right order.*

2 In 1876 Bartholdi travelled to the US to show his idea of the statue to the American people. They were very excited about it the arm alone was about 12 meters long! Bartholdi had also travelled to America to find the right place for the statue. He thought that the harbour of New York was perfect: This was where the people first arrived in the US and it would be the first thing they would see of the New World.

4 In 1884 Bartholdi and his workers finished the statue. But it was too big to put on a ship and send to the US. The statue's 300 pieces were put into 214 big boxes and sent to New York. But in New York the American people hadn't finished the statue's base[1]! They didn't have enough money and had to raise more before the work could go on. It took another two years until it was finished.

1 In 1865 a group of French people had the idea to build a statue and give it to the American people as a symbol of their friendship; the French wanted to give the Americans a 'birthday present' for the country's 100th birthday in 1876. But it took a few years longer until the present finally arrived in the US. Auguste Bartholdi wanted to build a statue that looked like a woman. But Bartholdi and the other French people needed a lot of money for their statue because they wanted it to be very big. They asked the French people for money and managed to raise enough for the statue. Bartholdi could finally begin work on the statue.

3 Bartholdi built his statue with copper, a metal which turns green after some time. But it was too difficult for him to build such a tall statue alone. That's why he asked the engineer Gustave Eiffel for help. (Gustave Eiffel? Have you ever heard of him? Yes, he later built the Eiffel Tower in Paris.) The work on the statue went on, and in 1878 the statue's face was finished and shown at the Paris World Exhibition.

5 In October 1886, almost ten years after America's 100th birthday, the Statue of Liberty on Liberty Island was given to the American people. With its 93 meters the statue can be seen from a long distance and for a long time it was the first thing many immigrants saw when they arrived in the US. They had come to the US in hope of freedom[2], liberty[3] and a new life – the statue was a symbol of it. Today the Statue of Liberty is an important tourist attraction. You can go to Liberty Island by ferry and climb the 354 steps inside the statue to get to the viewing windows in the crown.

[1]base [beɪs]= Fuß, Sockel • [2]freedom ['friːdəm]= Freiheit • [3]liberty ['lɪbəti] = Freiheit; Unabhängigkeit

c) *The Statue of Liberty tells her own story:* "Hello, my name is Statue of Liberty. I live in New York but I was born in France. My father was …" *Go on.*

1 Putting feelings into words

a) *Look at these faces. Match the feelings to the pictures:*

angry · bored · in love · excited

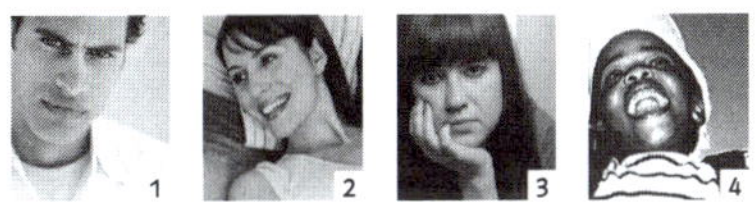

1 angry 2 in love 3 bored 4 excited

b) *Now have a look at these phrases. Which phrase belongs to which emotion?*

4 "I just can't believe it! Isn't it wonderful?"
3 "I'm sorry, I wasn't listening. What did you say?"
1 "I know that! You don't have to tell me!"
2/4 "You're a wonderful person!"
2/4 "He's absolutely fantastic!"
1 "Don't do that again!"
3 "What's the time?"
4 "It's fantastic!"
2 "He's so sweet!"

2 Idiomatic English

a) *On the left you find typical English idioms[1] which express emotions. Try to guess what they mean. Draw lines the correct sentences on the right.*

"He feels like a fish out of water!" · "He feels on top of the world!" · "He really needs to let off steam!" · "He's got ants in his pants!" · "He's head over heels in love!" · "He's proud as a peacock!" · "He could eat a horse!"

He's absolutely happy about something. · He feels uncomfortable in a situation. · He's very excited and can't sit still. · He's in love with someone and can't think of anything else. · He's very happy with himself, e. g. because he has won a competition. · He's so hungry he could eat anything. · He's angry or aggressive about something and needs to say or do something to get his mind off it.

[1]idiom ['ɪdiəm] = Redewendung

b) *Try to think of situations which are typical of the idioms.*

Example: You might feel like a fish out of water at a football stadium because you can't stand football.

3 Emotions, emotions, emotions

a) *Samantha calls her friend Gemma to tell her about something which happened to her. How does Samantha feel? Underline typical words and phrases in which she shows her feelings.*

"Hi Gemma. This is Sam. Something fantastic happened today! I want to tell you! You won't believe it. There's this boy from my sports club, Wayne. He's really nice. And he's cute, but I didn't think he even knew who I was. Today I met him on the bus. He was sitting in the back row. I didn't get a seat but I stood next to him. I said 'Hi'. He looked at me and said: 'Ah, I know you. You're in the judo club.' He'd forgotten my name but he knew who I was. Isn't that great? He knew who I was!!! And then we talked about judo and everything. But then guess what happened? All of a sudden the bus suddenly stopped and I fell onto him! Oh my God! It was so embarrassing! I think my head turned red. But he was so nice. He just laughed and smiled at me. I had to get off at the next stop but just before I left he said: 'Would you like to go to the movies with me tomorrow afternoon? There's a fantastic new movie about judo.' Wow, isn't that great? He wants to go to the movies with me. I can't believe it!"

b) *Now rewrite the text in a different emotion (e.g. sad). Change words and phrases, and change what has happened as well. Can your partner guess the emotion(s)?*

Friends

a) *Read the text from Dylan's diary and underline all the examples of the perfect infinitive in green. Then read it again and underline all examples of the passive infinitive in black.*

OK, OK. Maybe I should have invited Glenda to the movies on Friday. But she's always so jealous. I wouldn't have been able to talk to Allison at all. And why shouldn't I go out with Allison? She's just a friend! I'm not married to Glenda, but she always wants to be told about everything I do. She expects to be asked, too, wherever I go. She even comes to baseball practice with me! It's too much. She must be told: I'm a free man and we're not married! But how did she find out anyway? Phil must have told her. How could he have been so mean? He must have known that she'd go crazy. I'll have to call her. And she'll probably expect to be given a nice present or something. Girls! I'm better off without them.

b) *Now read Glenda's thoughts and write sentences with the perfect infinitive and the correct modal.*

Dylan *shouldn't have gone out* with Allison.

He *must have known* that I would find out.

He *needn't have worried* about me, though: I don't mind.

c) *Now read Glenda's conversation with Aileen and write sentences with the passive infinitive.*

Aileen: Yes, well. Dylan's very sweet, but I must say: He isn't a cool dude.

It must be said: Dylan isn't a cool dude.

Glenda: No, he even wants me to cheer for him at baseball practice.

No, he even *wants to be cheered* for at baseball practice.

Aileen: But why did you say yes when Joe asked you out?

Glenda: I was just so surprised. I wasn't expecting it.

I was just so surprised because *I wasn't expecting to be asked*.

Aileen: You should tell Dylan. Somebody might see you with Joe.

Dylan *should be told*. You *might be seen* with Joe.

Glenda: Oh no. I don't think I need to tell him everything. He can't expect that.

Oh no. I *can't be expected* to tell him everything.

When should British teenagers be allowed to drive?

a) *Read the text and put the paragraphs in the right order.*

A On the other hand it should be understood why young people are more likely[1] to have accidents than older people. It is partly because they have less experience as they haven't driven as long. If they learnt to drive when they were younger, they would become better at driving sooner. Also, if teenagers learnt to drive when they were still at home, their parents would be able to help them become careful drivers. When teenagers are allowed to be more independent, they behave more like intelligent adults, too.

B First and most importantly, it is well-known that more young drivers have accidents than older drivers. In 2009, for example, 26% of all accidents involved[2] young drivers (aged from 17 to 24). Young drivers have less experience than older drivers and so they have more accidents. Young people also take risks more often than older people. In cars these risks can kill other people.

C Teenagers should not be allowed to get their driver's license[3] until they are 17.

D In conclusion we know that driving on roads is dangerous, but children and young people have to do many things that are dangerous. I believe that teenagers should be able to get their driver's license when they are 16, so that they can learn to drive well sooner.

E Next, we should also ask ourselves if we want more cars on the road anyway. In Britain we have problems with the environment[4] and problems with overweight teenagers. People drive to shops when they could walk, cycle or take the bus. Teenagers don't need to be able to drive; they should use their legs. If people are allowed to drive when they are younger, they will get even less exercise, and there will be even more problems with our environment.

F Fifty years ago children became independent of their parents in Britain when they were 21. Soon after that the age changed and children became adults officially when they were 18. That is still true today. But although people are only seen as adults when they are 18, they are allowed to do many things earlier. Also, in many countries the laws are different, so the question is: When should teenagers be allowed to do what?

G Also, the law doesn't make sense. If British children have to cycle on the road, why should teenagers not be allowed to drive on it? It is well-known that cycling is very dangerous and many people die in bike accidents every year, but still the law allows children to cycle on the road. Surely, if they are expected to cycle, they should also be allowed to drive.

[1] likely ['laɪkli] = wahrscheinlich • [2] to involve [ɪn'vɒlv] = einschließen • [3] driver's license *(AE)* ['draɪvəz ˌlaɪsns] = Führerschein • [4] environment [ɪn'vaɪərnmənt] = Umwelt

Order: *C F B E A G D*

b) *Find the following words or phrases in the text.*

1. a phrase which contrasts something: *on the other hand*
2. two words which add information: *also, too*
3. two words and one phrase which put things in order: *first, next, in summary*
4. two words which give a reason: *because, as*

c) *Choose one of the topics below and write your own argumentative text.*

"Children should be allowed to leave school when they are 14."

"It's always a good thing to be tidy."

TIP Look at page 40 in your textbook.

Tandem activity: All's well that ends well[1]?

Partner A

a) *Sit back to back with Partner B. You both have pictures of a picture story, but you mustn't look at your partner's pictures. You have pictures 1, 3, 5 and 7 in the correct order. Your partner has the other missing pictures, but they're in the wrong order. Look at your pictures and describe them to your partner. Then listen to your partner. Find the correct order for all the pictures.*

b) *Look at the pictures with your partner and write the story as a short story or as a film script. Think about these questions:*

- What happened first?
- How did the man and woman get into that situation?
- What was their relationship?
- What happened at the end?
- Was the woman still alive?
- Did they become friends again?

Partner B

a) *Sit back to back with Partner A. You both have pictures of a picture story, but you mustn't look at your partner's pictures. You have pictures 2, 4, 6 and 8, but they're in the wrong order. Your partner has the other pictures in the right order. Listen to your partner. He/She must describe his/her picture first. Then describe your pictures to your partner. Find the correct order.*

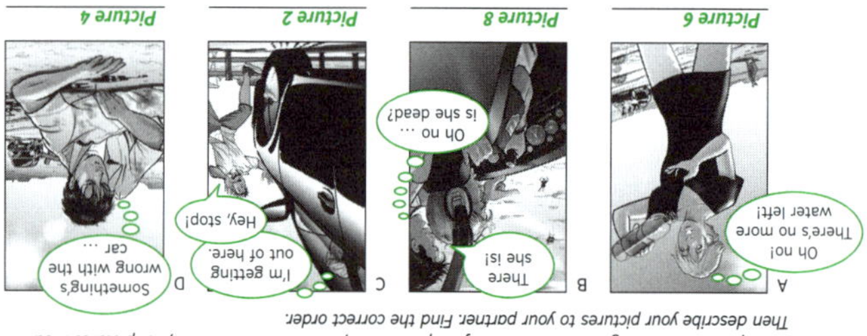

Picture 6 *Picture 8* *Picture 2* *Picture 4*

b) *Look at the pictures with your partner and write the story as a short story or as a film script. Think about these questions:*

- What happened first?
- How did the man and woman get into that situation?
- What was their relationship?
- What happened at the end?
- Was the woman still alive?
- Did they become friends again?

[1] All's well that ends well ['ɔːlz wel ðət ˌendz wel] = Ende gut, alles gut.

1 Revision: Passive or active voice

Have a look at the grid and fill in the missing active and passive sentences or tenses.

active	passive	tense
They produce crisps in this factory.	*Crisps are produced in this factory.*	*Simple present*
She's taking the dog for a walk.	*The dog is being taken for a walk.*	Present progressive
A bus hit her while she was crossing the road.	She was hit by a bus while she was crossing the road.	*Simple past*
The band was playing a beautiful song when we came in.	*A beautiful song was being played when we came in.*	*Past progressive*
They will build the house next summer.	The house will be built next summer.	*Will-future*
They haven't caught the burglars yet.	*The burglars haven't been caught yet.*	Present perfect
Two thieves had stolen the computer.	The computer had been stolen (by two thieves).	*Past perfect*

2 A very special lady

Turn these phrases into passive constructions. Can you guess who this very special lady is?

1. Christopher discovered her in the 15th century.
   She was discovered by Christopher in the 15th century.
2. White people took her land.
   Her land was taken by white people.
3. People from Mexico call her the El Dorado.
   She's called the EL Dorado by people from Mexico.
4. Since 2008 her first black president has governed her.
   She has been governed by her first black president since 2008.
5. France gave her a big statue as a present for her 100th birthday.
   She was given a big statue as a present by France.

Looking at … Polite language

a) *Look at these speech bubbles. Underline polite phrases in green and impolite phrases in black.*

No, I don't want to go. I'm tired.
Did you have a good day?
How are you doing?
Isn't it a nice day today?
Nice to meet you.
I'm not talking to you. Shut up.
Turn off your phone. It's giving me a headache.
Would you like to sit over here?
Would you like to drink something?
I'm sorry for taking up your time.
Get out of my way.
Thanks for helping me.
That sounds wonderful to me.
No, I didn't say that. You weren't listening.
I don't want that one. I want a bigger piece.
I don't have any time now. Come back later.

b) *Now try to turn the impolite phrases into polite ones.*

c) *Look at the German tourists in these pictures. They're in America and they all have a problem and need help. Turn their thoughts into polite phrases/questions.*

1.

2.

3.

4.

d) *What do the Americans answer? Write down little dialogues for these scenes.*

e) *Choose one of the situations and act it out with your partner.*

Looking at … Canyonlands National Park

Visit CANYONLANDS for the experience of a lifetime

Canyonlands is less known than other national parks in the US and therefore has fewer visitors than some of the more popular parks. Yellowstone has, for example, more than 2 million tourists every year; Canyonlands about 440,000 visitors. If you want to get away from it all and discover what the US was like hundreds of years ago, this is the place for you. It is also great for outdoor enthusiasts, and for people who love the colours of the desert.

Canyonlands is quite a new national park and was only created in 1964 (Yellowstone in 1872). It is a large area, split into four parts, where the Colorado and the Green Rivers meet in Utah. The weather is hot and dry with very little rain, with temperatures which are often over 30°C in summer. The park covers some of the least-visited areas in the US, and there are no roads between the different parts of the park. To visit large areas of the park you need a four-wheel drive or you have to travel on foot or by bike, taking the trails through the canyons. There are no shops in the park, but you can buy water at some of the visitors' centers.

Most visitors travel to the Island in the Sky area which is the easiest to get to. There is a visitors' center there and it's possible to go on hikes which only take a few hours. You can also go on walks together with park rangers. Camping is allowed at one of the official campsites, but only two cars and ten people at the most are allowed to stop at each one.

You can go climbing in the canyons, horse-riding along the trails or canoeing on the rivers. Canoeing is safe enough for the average canoeist on either of the rivers above their confluence, but only experienced canoeists should try canoeing on the water after the two rivers have met, as the river there becomes dangerously fast.

Another interesting part of the park is Horseshoe Canyon, where you can see paintings done over 3,000 to 4,000 years ago. These are some of the oldest paintings ever discovered in the United States. It should be remembered, however, that any paintings of horses must have been painted later, as there were no horses in North America 3,000 or 4,000 years ago.

a) *Read the text about Canyonlands National Park. Are the statements below true or false?*

	true	false
1. Not many people visit large areas of the park because it is difficult to travel around.	✔	
2. You are allowed to camp anywhere in the park if there are fewer than two cars together.		✔
3. Canoeing is only safe for experienced canoeists.		✔
4. Native Americans did not ride horses 4,000 years ago.	✔	

b) *Find words or phrases which mean the following:*

1. a person who loves life outdoors *outdoor enthusiast*
2. a kind of jeep which can travel off-road easily *four-wheel drive*
3. something which is not very good and not very bad *average*
4. the place where two rivers meet *confluence*

c) *Now write a short summary of the park in German for a friend who doesn't speak English.*

1 A trip to a national park

a) *Rewrite the marked clauses with an infinitive construction.*

When I saw the bear I didn't know **what I should do**.

When I saw the bear I didn't know what *to do.*

I wasn't sure whether **I should run or stand still**.

I wasn't sure whether *to run or stand still.*

I must be the only person **who tried to talk to a bear**.

I must be the only person *to try to talk to a bear.*

But I wasn't expecting **that the bear would reply**.

But I wasn't expecting *the bear to reply.*

b) *Now translate these sentences with the help of infinitive constructions.*

Ich wollte, dass eine Gruppe Freunde mit mir zum Yellowstone Park kommt.

I wanted a group of friends *to come with me to Yellowstone Park.*

Ich habe mich gefragt, wie viele Freunde ich mitnehmen soll.

I wondered how many *friends to take with me.*

Am Ende war Ellie die einzige Person, die ja sagte.

In the end Ellie was the only *person to say yes.*

Niemand erwartete, dass wir als mehr als gute Freunde zurückkommen würden.

Nobody expected *us to come back (as) more than good friends.*

2 Act a sentence

a) *Group work: In pairs, choose a sentence below and act it out. You can speak, but you mustn't use the words in the sentence. The other pairs should guess which sentence you were acting out. The first pair to guess gets a point. The pair with the most points is the winner.*

- They were climbing a mountain when they stopped to take a photo.
- They stopped taking photos when a rock fell down the mountain and almost hit them.
- He'd meant to check if there was a hole in the canoe before they left.
- They wanted to get back to the camp quickly but that meant carrying the canoe up the hill.
- When we saw the bear, we just went on walking.
- It was a great day. We saw a bear and then went on to walk twenty miles.
- He tried to call his dad, but his mobile wasn't working.
- He tried calling his dad, but his dad couldn't help them either.
- They didn't remember to take the trail which led to the left.
- They remembered walking up the trail which took them to the top of the cliff. What a great day!

b) *When you have acted out the above sentences, everybody should write their own sentences with a gerund or an infinitive.*

1 American or British English?

Find fifteen words in the wordsearch and write them in a grid under the headings AE or BE as below. Then complete the grid with the American or British equivalent and the German translation.

AE	BE	German
apartment	flat	Wohnung
garbage	rubbish	Müll
center	centre	Zentrum
highway	motorway	Autobahn
cell phone	mobile	Handy
check	bill	Rechnung
subway	underground	U-Bahn
railroad	railway	Eisenbahn
pants	trousers	Hose
vacation	holiday	Urlaub
candy	sweets	Süßigkeiten
fall	autumn	Herbst
jewelry	jewellery	Schmuck
store	shop	Geschäft
fries	chips	Pommes frites

B	A	P	A	R	T	M	E	N	T
R	U	B	B	I	S	H	J	P	L
S	T	C	E	N	T	R	E	C	X
W	U	T	H	I	G	H	W	A	Y
E	M	M	O	B	I	L	E	B	F
E	N	Q	B	I	L	L	L	S	R
T	S	U	B	W	A	Y	R	T	I
S	R	A	I	L	W	A	Y	O	E
O	P	A	N	T	S	U	T	R	S
V	H	O	L	I	D	A	Y	E	E

2 A crossword

Complete the crossword.

1. They would remember that day forever. It was …
2. The trail was very … There wasn't enough room for two people to walk side-by-side.
3. That film isn't scary. It's too … You always know what's going to happen.
4. You need some … in yourself to climb that cliff – it's no good if you're nervous.
5. Somebody who takes too many risks is …
6. When you … something, you finally understand it without anybody telling you.
7. Trees are tall, and rivers are … – the water goes down a long way.
8. A … is a person who kills animals in forests, for example, when they aren't allowed to.
9. When you leave school before you pass your exams, you … early.
10. A … is a small path which usually is quite long.
11. A … is a book which tells a story.
12. If you don't think or care about other people or animals, you are …

	1 U										
	2 N	A	R	R	O	W			3 P		
	F								R		
4 C	O	N	F	I	D	E	N	C	E		
	R								D		5 R
	G				6 R	E	A	L	I	Z	E
7 D	E	E	8 P						C		C
	T		O			9 Q	U	I	T		K
	10 T	R	A	I	L				A		L
	A		C						B		E
	B		H		11 N	O	V	E	L		S
	L		E						E		S
12 H	E	A	R	T	L	E	S	S			

3 Word families

How many words do you know in these word families? Write them down in your exercise book.

end | camp | care | help | usual | fear | back | beauty

TIP
You can use compound nouns, too.

Hollywood stars

Read these texts about famous stars.

a) *Fill in the correct relative pronouns and underline the relative clauses. Put commas where necessary.*

b) *Can you guess who the stars are?*

This English actor **, who** also worked as a model, musician and producer, was born in London in 1986. He had already acted in two movies when he played the role of Cedric Diggory in the fourth Harry Potter movie "The Goblet of Fire". The movies **which/that** made him famous, however, were the "Twilight"-movies. He played the role of Edward Cullen, a vampire **who** falls in love with the teenage girl Bella Swan.

R [17]O B E R T P A T T I N [15]S O N

This former child star is one of the first music stars **who/that** became famous via the Internet. The pop singer and songwriter **, who** now lives in Hollywood, was born in Canada in 1994. His mum **, who** always supported his interest in music, uploaded some videos on YouTube. Scooter Brown **, who** works for a big record company, saw the videos and liked the young boy and his show.

J U [8]S T I N B I [6]E B E [11]R

This American actor **, who** has been described as one of the world's most attractive men, was born in 1963. He had already played in quite a lot of movies in the 1980s before he made movies like "Thelma & Louise", "Interview with the Vampire", "Seven", or "Fight Club" **, which** made him really famous. Between 2001 and 2007 he played together with George Clooney **, who** is one of his close friends, in the "Ocean's" series.

B R [1]A [3]D P I [4]T [16]T

She was a blonde American actress, singer, model and showgirl **who** played in a number of successful movies in the 1950s. The real name of the actress, **, who** was born in 1926, was Norma Jean Baker, but in the 1940s she took on a new name **, which** made her famous. She played in films like "Some Like it Hot" or "How to Marry a Millionaire" **, which** earned her a lot of fame. She was married three times and is said to have had an affair with John F. Kennedy **, who** was American President at that time. She died in 1962 in her home in Los Angeles at the age of 36.

M A R I L Y [2]N M [7]O N R O [14]E

This American actress **, who** was born in 1984, became a star when she was still very young. In 1994 at the age of nine she acted in the film "North" **, which** was her first role ever. In 1998 she acted with Robert Redford in the film "The Horse Whisperer" which gained her a Young Star Award. She played girls or teenagers in a lot of other films before she switched to adult roles. In 2003 she acted the leading role in "Lost in Translation" **, which** was the second big film by the director Sophia Coppola and was a big success for both – for the director and for the leading actress.

S [9]C [10]A R L E T T
J [5]O H A N S S [13]O N

c) *Put the letters in the boxes. The little numbers help you with the right order. The solution sentence is one of the most popular sentences in Hollywood.*

[1]A [2]N [3]D [4]T [5]H [6]E
[7]O [8]S [9]C [10]A [11]R [12]G [13]O [14]E [15]S [16]T [17]O

d) *Make your own quiz about a famous star and let your partner guess who it is.*

Green Line 3/4
Vertretungsstunden
ISBN: 978-3-12-560036-2

1 Elements of a story

Match the elements with the right definition. Write the right number in the boxes.

1 setting | 2 genre | 3 plot | 4 character | 5 atmosphere | 6 narrator

The storyline or events which happen in a novel, film, drama, etc. **3**	A person in a drama, novel, film etc. There are main ones who are very important and less important ones. **4**	Category or kind of literature or film, e.g. comedy, tragedy, love story, western, etc. **2**
A person who tells a story. He/She tells it from his/her perspective and can be a character in the story. **6**	Describes the mood or tone of the story. It can be sad, scary, etc. – this is often done with the help of adjectives. **5**	The time and place when and where a drama, novel, film, etc. takes place, for example the story might be set in New York in the 1920s. **1**

2 Be the author – write the story

a) *Match the right elements. Which elements belong to which genres? Write down the right numbers.*

Genre	(1) Western	(2) Science Fiction	(3) Love Story	(4) Crime Story
Setting	**place:** planet Ulysses, **time:** in the year 2454 **2**	**place:** American high school in Phoenix, Arizona **time:** end of school year, 2013 **3**	**place:** Coxton, a small town in Nevada in the American West **time:** 1890s, hot summer **1**	**place:** Chicago, big city **time:** 1920s, foggy November **4**
Characters	**Amber**, 15 years old, a shy, clever student **Jacob**, 16 years old and very sporty **Amy**, 15 years old, very attractive but arrogant **3**	**Detective Wallace**, 63 years old, experienced detective **Warren Ellis**, 29 years old, his young and ambitious sergeant **4**	**John Walker**, good sheriff, wants to fight bandits[1] and villains[2] and protect[3] people **Gene McLain**, the villain, he robs people and is violent **1**	**Henoto**, the leader of the Hawks on planet Ulysses **Tyranto**, the leader of the Cheerios **Tiffylio**, the son of Tyranto, a strong fighter **2**
Plot	A dead body of a young man has been found near the Chicago River. Detective Wallace and Sergeant Ellis have arrived at the scene of crime. The dead body was the young lover of a rich old lady … **4**	The new sheriff John Walker arrives in the small town of Coxton. The villain Gene McLain isn't happy about that. He isn't seen for some days. But trains are robbed on their way to Coxton and one day McLain returns … **1**	People are running out of water on planet Ulysses; but they need water to survive, there is a war between the Hawks and the Cheerios about who has the power[4] over the water … **2**	Amber is secretly in love with Jacob. He likes her but doesn't know that she's in love with him. Amy has found out that Amber loves Jacob and wants to go out with him so that Amber won't get him … **3**

[1]bandit [ˈbændɪt] = Bandit • [2]villain [ˈvɪlən] = Schurke • [3]protect [prəˈtekt] = (be)schützen • [4]power [ˈpaʊə] = Macht

b) *Now choose one of the stories and write it.*

Green Line 3/4
Vertretungsstunden
ISBN: 978-3-12-560036-2

Green Line 3

Unit 1

KV 1 1 Famous athletes: A quiz

b) 1. Usain Bolt is the sprinter who holds the world record in the 100- and 200- metre sprints.
2. Roger Federer is the tennis player who won 32 tennis matches in 2008 and didn't lose one.
3. Lionel Messi is the football player who plays for the FC Barcelona and is the captain of the Argentina national team.
4. Serena Williams is the tennis player from America who has won more than 26 Grand Slam titles.
5. Dirk Nowitzki is the basketball player who plays for the Dallas Mavericks and who is 2.13 m tall.
6. Michael Phelps is the American swimmer who has won more than 15 Olympic gold medals.
7. Lindsey Vonn is an American ski racer who has won 50 world cup races in her career.
8. Sebastian Vettel is the Formula 1 driver who was world champion in 2010 and 2011.

KV 2 1 Working as a football reporter

c) *Lösungsvorschläge:*
commentator: A commentator is someone who explains what is happening in a match. He/She works for TV or radio stations.
stadium: A stadium is the place where the football match takes place. Many people can sit or stand there and watch the game.
to kick off: to start a match with a first kick
whistle: The referee blows his whistle when there's been a foul or when the match is over.
penalty shot: When a player has fouled somebody, the other team gets a penalty shot, which gives them the chance to score a goal.
to miss: When a player misses the ball, he tries to kick it but can't.
defender: A defender is a player whose job is to keep the ball out of his team's goal.
half: A football match has two halves; one half is usually 45 minutes long.
midfielder: A midfielder is a player whose position is in the middle of the football field.

2 Germany plays England: Write your own football report

a) + b) *Lösungsvorschlag:*
Hello, this is Peter Brooke from the BBC. We're here at Wembley Stadium, London. Welcome to this match between England and Germany. The game starts, Germany kicks off.
The score is still nil–nil after 17 minutes at Wembley Stadium. But now Rooney has got the ball and scores. Goal. Gooooooooaaaaaaaal for England! A beautiful goal by Wayne Rooney in the 17th minute. The German goalkeeper Manuel Neuer tried to get the ball but no chance. One–nil for England.
The score is still one–nil here after 43 minutes at Wembley stadium, London. Ashley Cole from the English team has got the ball, but now Thomas Müller from the German team comes towards him. He tries to get the ball. But what's he doing now? Cole is attacked

by Müller, a terrible foul by Müller. What is the referee going to do? He's seen it and blows his whistle. Yellow card for Müller!
After 52 minutes of the match the score is still one–nil for England. But now Germany's Lukas Podolski has got the ball. And he is fast and running towards England's goalkeeper Joe Hart. He shoots the ball and he misses the goal. Oh, bad luck for Podolski, but England is happy. The score is still one–nil after 81 minutes. Germany's captain Philipp Lahm has got the ball but England's midfielder James Milner comes from the right. He hits the ball – oh, he doesn't hit the *ball*, he hits *Lahm*! Oh, that's a foul. Milner, what are you doing there? The referee has seen it, it's a yellow card for Milner and, yes, it's a penalty shot for Germany.
Who'll shoot the penalty? Ah, it's Philipp Lahm himself. He shoots and – gooooaaaaaal, goal for Germany! So now the score is one–one here at Wembley Stadium London.
And that was the referee's whistle: After 92 minutes the game is over. One–one. A beautiful game with two strong teams.

KV 3 Looking at … Football

b) *Lösungsvorschlag:*
BC: Ball games existed in many cultures around the world, like ancient Greece and Rome, Australia or China. The players were often allowed to use their hands.
Middle Ages: Football was popular in England but the rules were very different from our football rules today. Two villages often played against each other.
18th and 19th century: Football was popular among the students at England's public schools. Many teachers didn't want the boys to play football, but Thomas Arnold thought it was a good idea.
1848: The first football rules were written down by boys at Cambridge University. However, they were still very different from our rules today.
1857: FC Sheffield became the world's first football club.
1874: The teacher Konrad Koch brought football to Germany.

c) *Lösungsvorschlag:*
Dear Thomas, I'm now at Eaton College in … *(eigene Schülerlösung)* At school we study hard but in our free time we often play a new game. It's called football and it's really fun. For football you need two teams. There are 15 to 20 players in each team and there is one ball. The ball is made of leather but it's filled with air so it's very light. Normally the teams wear shirts in different colours so that you know who plays in which team. There are two goals at the right and left side of the pitch. You must try to get the ball into the other team's goal. But you're only allowed to use your feet. Each team has a goalkeeper. He tries to catch the ball before it hits the goal and he can use his hands. It's really fun and we enjoy the game. Usually we play for 45 minutes, have a little break and then play another 45 minutes. You should come and visit me in the summer holidays. Then you can play in our team.
Yours,
James

Unit 2

KV 1 A trip to a museum

a) Class 9a were allowed to take photos, but they weren't allowed to take the Roman money with them. They had to leave the museum at 5pm.They were able to wear a Roman soldier's uniform, but they weren't able to walk in it. They weren't allowed to use the Roman's toilets.

b) *Lösungsvorschlag:*
Most Roman children had to work and I don't have to work.
Many Roman children didn't have to go to school, but I have to go to school.
I have to do homework every day, but they didn't have to do homework.
I am able to use the bathroom in my house; most Roman children weren't able to use a bathroom because they didn't have one.
They weren't able to go on holiday every year, but I can.

d) The pupils from Class 9a and their teacher are on the bus on the way back to school. They had been to a museum about the Romans. One girl had spent all her money; now she's wondering where her money is! Two boys had fought each other; now they're not speaking to each other. One boy had bought a book about Romans. The teacher had lost his mobile; you can see that he can't find it. A boy and girl had fallen in love; you can see that they *really* like each other!

KV 2 Looking at … A famous person in history

c) *Lösungsvorschlag:*
Florence Nightingale lived a long time ago. She was beautiful but she didn't want to get married. She wanted to become a nurse and work in a hospital. She went to Germany and trained to become a nurse. Her mum was angry with her but she knew that God wanted her to do it. She got upset when people died and she found it very hard, but she became a nurse in the end.
Later she went to look after soldiers who were fighting. They called her the lady with the lamp because she went to look after the soldiers every night with a lamp in her hand.

d) *Lösungsvorschlag:*
Frances was Florence's sister. She wasn't as beautiful as Florence. She wanted to marry a man who was called James. She stayed friends with her sister.
Theodor was German and he was very kind and gentle. He taught people how to become nurses and look after other people. He also taught people how to stay clean and that it was important to wash their hands often.
Henry was a soldier who lost one of his legs in the war. He wrote letters home to his girlfriend, Jenny. Florence Nightingale was his nurse.

Unit 3

KV 3 1 All about Michelle

b) *Lösungsvorschlag:*
Meine Mutter **hat mich** um 6:30 Uhr **geweckt** und dann **bin ich aufgestanden**, **habe mich angezogen** und dann gefrühstückt. Danach bin ich mit dem Bus zur Schule gefahren. In der Schule haben wir einen Vokabeltest geschrieben. **Ich habe mich geärgert**, weil ich einige Vokabeln nicht wusste …
Nach der Schule bin ich nach Hause gefahren und habe zu Mittag gegessen. Nach den Hausaufgaben **habe ich mich** mit meinem Freund Andreas **getroffen**. **Wir haben uns** in einem Café **ein Eis gekauft**, **haben uns unterhalten** und hatten viel Spaß! Ich ging um 8:00 Uhr nach Hause und sah noch etwas fern. Um 10:00 Uhr bin ich ins Bett gegangen.

My mother woke me up at 6:30. I got up, got dressed and had breakfast. After that I went to school by bus. At school we took a vocabulary test. I was angry with myself because I didn't know all the words …
After school I went home and had lunch. After my homework I met my friend Andreas. We **bought**

ourselves an ice-cream at a café, talked and really **enjoyed ourselves**! I went home at 8 o'clock and watched TV. I went to bed at 10 o'clock.

2 The Patterson family

b) *Lösungsvorschlag:*
What would you have done if there had been no school today?
What will you do if you do badly in the next English test?
What would you do if you met a nice boy/girl?

c) *Lösungsvorschlag:*
If there'd been no school today, I'd have stayed in bed until 9 am.
If I do badly in the next English test, I'll listen to more English music.
If I met a nice boy/girl, I wouldn't tell anybody.

KV 2 An argument

c) *Lösungsvorschlag:*

Ella: Hi Jeanie! I was a bit sad that you didn't call me on Saturday. Did something go wrong?
Jeanie: Oh, but I *did* call you. Didn't your parents tell you? They told me that you had already gone out.
Ella: Oh, no they didn't tell me. When did you call?
Jeanie: I called at about 7pm. We were really late back from the hike because we'd got lost, but I called you as soon as I got home.
Ella: Oh, I'm sorry. I thought you'd decided to go out with Harvey. And then Jack called and invited me to the cinema. I said yes because I was so angry with you. I'm really sorry about that.
Jeanie: Oh, don't worry about it. I'm sorry that I didn't call you earlier. I would have called you if I'd remembered to take my mobile.

KV 4 2 A play: Messages gone wrong!

b) *Lösungsvorschlag:*

Answering machine: Hello, we're sorry, but we can't answer the phone just now. Please leave a message after the tone and we'll call you back.
Corey: Hi Mum, Dad. It's me. I'll be late home this evening because I'm going to Taylor's to do my homework. We've got lots of Maths homework over the weekend. See you later.
Ashley: But what if your parents call Taylor? They'll know that you're not there and then you'll be in trouble.
Corey: Yes, I'll call Taylor. *(sound of buttons and then ringing)*
Taylor's mum: Hello, this is 354 6757.
Corey: Hello Mrs Johnson. Is Taylor there?
Taylor's Mum: No, sorry. He's not back from school yet. Do you want me to take a message?
Corey: Yes, please. Could you ask him to call me back on my mobile?
Taylor's mum: Yes, of course. Bye.
Corey: Thanks Mrs Johnson. Good bye.
(Corey and Ashley arrive at his house.)
Corey: And are your parents going to be out all evening?
Ashley: Yes, they won't be back until about 12:00. Do you want something to eat?
(sound of people arriving and music)
(A phone rings)
Ashley: Corey! Corey! Your mobile's ringing. Where is he? It might be his parents – I'll answer it. Hello!
Taylor: Hello? Who's that?
Ashley: It's Ashley. Oh, hi Taylor.
Taylor: Where's Corey? He wanted me to call him back.
Ashley: I don't know where he is now. He's in the house somewhere. But do you want to come around? My parents are out, so I'm having a party.
Taylor: Yes. Thanks. See you in a bit.
Ashley: See you.
(Everybody's dancing etc and the door bell rings)
Ashley: Will you open the door Corey? It's probably Taylor.
(opens door; Corey's mum is at the door, looking very angry and Taylor is behind her)
Corey: Er. Hello, Mum.
Corey's mum: *(very loudly)* And what do you think you're doing here when you said that …
Corey: Mum, not so loud! Everybody can hear you.
Corey's mum: I don't care if everybody can hear me!

Unit 4

KV 1 2 Tandem activity: How to help people

a) *Lösungsvorschläge:*

Situation 1:

Chris: Excuse me, can I help you?
Maureen: Oh, yes, thank you. I've just arrived by train here at Peterborough Station. I want to visit my son. He lives in Bourne, but Bourne doesn't have a train station and he said that I need to take a bus. But I forgot which bus I must take …
Chris: Don't worry, I can help you. We can look at the map over there.
Maureen: Oh, could you do that for me? I don't have my glasses with me.
Chris: Yes, of course. No problem. Let's see. Mmmhhh … you need to take the 101 or the 102. The next one leaves at quarter to five.
Maureen: Oh thank you very much. But where does it leave?
Chris: It leaves over there at Queensgate Bay 4. Can I show you the way?
Maureen: Oh, that's very kind of you. Thank you.
Chris: Here we are. Your bus will come in about 10 minutes.
Maureen: Thank you very much. You've been a great help.

Situation 2:

Keira: Hello! Can I help you?
Kristen: Hello, Keira. Is your mum at home?
Keira: No, she isn't. She'll be back home this evening.
Kristen: Hmm, that'll be to late … I have a little problem: I have to go to work and the baby sitter can't come to look after Jason because she's ill.
Keira: Maybe I can help you and look after him. I really like Jason!
Kristen: Hm, I don't know, Keira. That's really very nice of you, but you're still a bit young …
Keira: Oh, don't worry, I've looked after my little cousins lots of times. I'm sure that I can do it.
Kristen: Well, OK, then. Thank you very much for your help, Keira. Could you come over in half an hour?
Keira: Of course. I'm glad I can help!
Kristen: Great! See you later!
Keira: Bye!

Situation 3:

Steven: Hi Mike, I wanted to ask you something. Do you remember that party we went to two weeks ago?
Mike: Hey Steven. Of course I remember that. It was a great party, wasn't it?
Steven: Yes, it was … Do you remember the girl I talked to?
Mike: Hmm, I don't know. What's her name?
Steven: Her name is Jasmine. She had long, brown hair and was very pretty. But I don't have her phone number. I think she's a friend of your sister

Emily, so I thought I'd ask you if you could help me …

Mike: Oh yes, I know Jasmine. She's very nice. I don't have her number, but I can ask Emily about it if you want to.
Steven: Yes, that'd be great! Thanks a lot, Mike!
Mike: No problem, mate!

3 A new pupil

a) *Lösungsvorschlag:*
He's probably a little scared because he doesn't know anyone and everything at school will be so new. He might also feel sad because he had to leave his old school and his old friends. He might also be a little bit excited; a new school is a place for new friends!

b) *Lösungsvorschläge:*
They can be very friendly and ask him if he needs help.
They can show him the new school so that he won't get lost.
They can take him to his classes.
They can sit next to him in class.
They can play games with him in the break or talk to him.
They can invite him to do something fun with them after school.
They can invite him to their birthday party.

c) *Lösungsvorschlag:*
Rhona: Hi Simon. Nice to meet you. I'm Rhona and this is Shirin. We're both in your tutor group. Welcome to our school.
Simon: Oh thank you very much. It's so big …
Shirin: Yes, it is. I remember when I was here on my first day of school I got completely lost. I wanted to go to the language department and in the end I found the cafeteria. This school is so big.
Simon: Ah, so you're new as well.
Shirin: Well, my family moved here about one year ago. We used to live in Manchester and then my dad got a new job in Swansea so we had to move. I know what it feels like to be at a new school.
Simon: It's a bit strange. Everything is new, the teachers, the students and the building …
Rhona: If you want to we can show you around the school at lunch break.
Simon: Oh, yes, that would be great. Thank you very much. That's cool.
Rhona: No problem. You're welcome.
Simon: I've got P.E. now, but I don't know how to get to the gym. Can you show me the way?
Shirin: Oh, just come with us. We've got P.E. too. It's this way.
Simon: Ah great. Thanks.

KV 2 Looking at … A Pakistani family

a) 1958: Shirin's granparents got married in Pakistan.
1960: Aunt Zeba was born.
1961: The family moved to Britain.
1970: Shirin's father was born. He is the youngest child of the family.
1992: Shirin's father and mother met at a restaurant.
1995: Shirin's parents got married.
1997: Shirin was born.
Today: Shirin lives with her parents in Swansea and visits her aunt in Manchester.

b)
- The wedding photo doesn't look like a wedding photo to Rhona because Shirin's grandparents wear traditional Punjabi clothes.
- He went to Britain because life in Pakistan was hard and he hoped to earn more money.
- Pakistan was a former colony of Britain.
- Aunt Zeba calls Shirin's father "the baby" because he's the youngest child of the family.
- Aunt Zeba had a problem when she went to primary school because she didn't speak any English at first.
- It's their language and culture.
- She was scared because she thought that Shirin's grandparents might not like her because many Pakistani families want their sons to marry Pakistani women.
- Britain has become her home.

KV 3 1 Reading factual texts

a) The text is about mountain safety rules in Mount Snowdon and Snowdonia National Park.

c) *Lösungsvorschlag:*
- Watch the weather forecast before you go.
- Take warm clothes – the weather on the mountain top is usually colder.
- Don't wear any jeans – they dry too slowly.
- Wear good hiking boots.
- Bring extra food and drink.
- Bring a map and a compass and be able to use them.
- Bring a mobile phone to call for help.
- Let people know when and where you go.
- Bring a whistle and a torch.

2 Rhona's adventure in the mountains

a) *Lösungsvorschläge:*
- They probably didn't watch the weather forecast.
- They didn't bring any extra clothes and only had their T-shirts.
- They wore jeans, and jeans don't dry very quickly.
- They didn't take a map to look up the way.
- They didn't take their mobiles to call for help.

b) *Lösungsvorschlag:*
Mum was really angry with dad. She even shouted at him. Well, but of course that didn't change anything. We looked at the path we had come up the mountain on and we looked at the side. Both paths were very steep. Mum was really scared and told dad that she wouldn't be able to go down this mountain. Dad didn't know what to do. Suddenly another person appeared at the top. His name was Chris and he was from England. He had lost the way when he saw us and thought that we were on the right track. When he arrived at the top he realized that we didn't know the way. But he had a lot of experience with climbing and he had some good equipment. First we ate some of his extra food and he also gave us some water. Then he helped us to get down the mountain – we had to go very slowly, but with the help of Chris and dad even mum managed to get down. We arrived at the youth hostel when it was almost getting dark. What an adventure!

Unit 5

KV 1 Looking at … Soaps in Britain

c) *Lösungsvorschlag:*
"Gute Zeiten, schlechte Zeiten" is a German soap opera which is produced by the German company „Grundy UFA“. It has been on TV since 1992 and is the most popular soap opera in Germany. It's shown on RTL five times a week. "GZSZ", as it is called by its fans, is filmed in Germany's capital Berlin. The characters in this soap are mostly young: Some of them still go to school, some study and some of them are new in their jobs. The soap tells about the problems they have with money, relationships, school, work, etc.
Many of the new characters leave the soap again after a little while, but some of the characters have been on the soap for a very long time, some even from the very beginning.

So far there have been more than 4,000 episodes and the soap will probably be just as popular is the coming years as it is today.

KV 2 1 Media and more!

b) *Lösungsvorschlag:*

This is like one big computer that is used by people all over in the world. Information is kept here and can be downloaded onto home or office computers. Also apps can be found here that can be used by people in many different countries, for example programs which translate words.

Many things are bought and sold on this website every day. A description and a picture of a product is given and you can say how much you'd like to buy it for. The product is given to the person who offers the most money.

This is very old but it is still used by many people in the whole world in many different places. For example, it is listened to in cars or in houses or even on the computer.

These are TV shows that are often shown every day or twice or three times a week. They are usually about families who live in a certain place. They are made and shown in many countries in the world.

2 Media!

The media are used for information and communication. A kind of newspaper was used thousands of years ago by the Romans. Information was written out in the market place in Rome. Romans read about great battles which had been won by Julius Caesar. Hundreds of years later newspapers and books were made out of paper.

Plays were also an early form of media. Plays were performed in towns all over the world. They were watched for entertainment but also for information. With the invention of television and radio, entertainment and information could be got by a much larger audience. Also people were informed more quickly about what happened in other parts of the world.

In the last fifty years communication has been greatly improved by modern technology. Our whole lifestyle has been changed by the modern media. How will it be changed by new inventions in the future?

3 A party for the stars

b) 1. A rich actor sent an invitation to many important directors and actors.
   - Many important directors and actors were sent an invitation by a rich actor.
   - An invitation was sent to many important directors and actors by a rich actor.

2. He made wonderful food for his guests.
   - Wonderful food was made for his guests.
   - His guests were made wonderful food.

4. At the end of the evening a director offered the rich actor a great role in a new film.
   - At the end of the evening the rich actor was offered a great role in a new film by a director.
   - At the end of the evening a great role in a new film was offered to the rich actor by a director.

6. In the last few years other directors have promised him good roles.
   - In the last few years he has been promised good roles by other directors.
   - In the last few years good roles have been promised to him by other directors.

KV 3 1 Advertisements

	1. Which people use these products most or go to these places?	2. Which adjectives describe the products or places?	3. What else is often connected with these products or places?
A television:	everybody but mainly men	modern, new, exciting, fun, high quality	entertainment, family evening, fun evening with friends
Sun cream:	everybody but mainly younger women and children	safe, healthy, water-proof	hot places, beaches, swimming pools, the sea
Mobile phone:	young men and women	modern, fast, easy-to-use, cool	Internet, music, friends
Holiday in Majorca:	young men and women, old men and women	fun, beautiful, exciting, interesting, hot	sea, friends, cycling, walking, good weather
Car:	middle-aged and older men	fast, cool, attractive, safe	music, trips, foreign countries
Make-up:	younger women	beautiful, natural, colourful, water-proof	friends, water, discos
Soft drink:	young men and women	sweet, tasty	sport, beach, hot places
Holiday in Greece:	everybody	exciting, interesting, hot, fun, friendly	beaches, Greek food, sea, islands

2 Tandem activity: Find the products

a) + b) *Lösungsvorschläge:*

make-up: A woman and a man are standing in front of a swimming pool. They're probably on holiday. The woman has just got out of the pool. She looks happy and beautiful. A man is giving her a drink. The slogan says: "Be beautiful … any time!"

car: A man is driving a car and a woman is sitting next to him. A man is behind them on a donkey. They're on holiday somewhere near the sea. The woman and man look happy and the car looks new. The slogan says: "Powerful, fast, safe – wherever you want to go."

mobile: A young man is taking a photo of a group of teenagers. They're in the park and they all look happy.

You can see a city behind them. A girl has a mobile in her hand and is looking at it. The slogan says: "For the best moments of your life!"
holiday in Spain: Four teenagers are in a bar. A man is giving them something to eat on a small plate. He looks friendly and the four teenagers are listening to him. They all look happy. The slogan says: "Spend a great time with new friends!"

c) *Lösungsvorschlag:*
Partner A: I don't think ad 1 is a good ad. When I think of Majorca, I think of beaches and the sea.
Partner B: Yes, but maybe this shows a different side of Majorca. This says, "Come to Majorca and have fun with us." It wants to speak to a different group of people – young people, who want to have fun but don't want to lie on the beach all day.
Partner A: Maybe, but it could be anywhere. It's not special.

KV 4 2 General knowledge: The Internet!

c) *Antworten Stand August 2012:*
1. 130; 2. 465 million; 3. 4 billion; 4. 1,000 years; 5. 22 million; 6. 845 million; 7. 20; 8. 77

Unit 6

KV 4 1 On holiday on the Isle of Wight

b) 1. Glen asked how long Sally was staying on the island.
Sally replied that they were staying until the following Saturday.
2. Sally asked if he had ever been there before.
Glen answered that he had been there two years before.
3. Glen asked where she had gone yesterday.
Sally said that they had gone to Steephill Cove.
4. Glen asked what the weather would be like the following day.
Sally replied that it would be windy but cold.
5. Glen asked whether you could go surfing on that island.
Sally advised him to go to the west of the island if he wanted to go surfing; the waves were better there.
6. Sally asked if he would like to go surfing with them the following day.
Glen replied that that would be great, but he couldn't surf.

2 Report a dialogue

Lösungsvorschlag:
(S. 44: Sunday lunch)
Dad asked when the last time had been that they had eaten Sunday lunch together. Mum said she couldn't remember and then asked if Jake was still in bed. He had come home very late the night before. Amy said that he hadn't enjoyed himself at all because he had split up with Miriam. Mum was surprised and said that she had liked Miriam and that she would call Jake on her mobile. She then asked Jake if he was OK and said that lunch was ready. Dad said that he would put the meat on the plates and that everyone could help themselves to vegetables. Amy said that she didn't want any meat because she had decided to become a vegetarian.

KV 2 Tandem activity: Small talk openers

a) openers:
It's a beautiful day today, isn't it?
The bus is late again. It's typical, isn't it? And then three come at the same time!
Are you on holiday here, too?
What cool music! Do you know who it is?
A bit cold today, isn't it?
Don't I know you from somewhere?

responses:
Er, I don't know. I don't think I know you.
Oh no. I think it's quite warm actually.
Oh, I don't really like it. I don't like techno.
Oh, I think the buses are quite good in Liverpool.
Yes, I am. We arrived on Saturday.
Yes, it is. It's been nice for a few days, hasn't it?

b) It's a beautiful day today, isn't it?
– Yes, it is. It's been nice for a few days, hasn't it?

The bus is late again. It's typical, isn't it? And then three will come at once!
– Oh, I think the buses are quite good in Liverpool.

Are you on holiday here, too?
– Yes, I am. We arrived on Saturday.

What cool music! Do you know who it is?
– Oh, I don't really like it. I don't like techno.

A bit cold today, isn't it?
– Oh no. I think it's quite warm actually.

Don't I know you from somewhere?
– Er, I don't know. I don't think I know you.

c) *Lösungsvorschläge:*
1. I'm really excited. I hope there are some tickets left when we get to the front./Have you ever been to one of their concerts before?
2. It's really full again today, isn't it?/Would you like to sit here?
3. I'm not sure if I like the art here, or if I don't understand it. What about you?/Do you like this painting? I think it's beautiful.
4. He's really funny, isn't he?
Have you ever seen him here before?

d) *Lösungsvorschlag:*
You: I went to Majorca last year but I didn't like it at all.
Partner: Oh no. Why not?
You: Well, it is a beautiful island but there are just too many tourists – especially German and English tourists.
Partner: Oh, I see.
You: Yes, and you meet them everywhere you go and I want to see a different country with different people in it when I go on holiday.
Partner: Yes, I know what you mean.
You: And they always change the food when there are lots of tourists in a place, don't they?
Partner: I don't know really.

KV 3 Looking at ... Transport in Britain

d) *Lösungsvorschläge:*
Text B (advertisement):
Free travel in Manchester!
Don't bring your car to Manchester – you can travel free on the No. 1 and No. 2 buses all around the centre of Manchester.
And remember: If you're over 60, you can travel free on all buses and on the Metrolink.
Check our website for details: tfgm.co.uk.

Text C (e-mail):
Hi Rachel,
It was great to meet you in Brighton today, but I got home really late. It was terrible. First I missed the train at 6:17 pm and then I couldn't get the next train at 6:34 because it was a different train company. I couldn't believe it. It was because I'd bought the wrong return ticket – you can't use them with different companies. So I was late home and mum was angry because she knew I had a test the next day. The test went really badly. Stupid trains!
Anyway, see you next week.
Tim

Green Line 4

Unit 1

KV 2 Looking at … The Statue of Liberty

c) *Lösungsvorschlag:*
"Hello, my name is Statue of Liberty. I live in New York but I was born in France. My father was Auguste Bartholdi. He had the idea to build a statue that looks like a woman – me. He and some other French people wanted to give me as a present to the American people for the 100th birthday of the United States. But Dad and the other French people didn't have enough money so it took them a long time to build me. Dad decided to build me of copper – that's why I look so green today. And then he needed some help because he wanted to build me very high and so he asked my uncle Gustave Eiffel, who later built my cousin, the Eiffel Tower, for help. In 1876 Dad went to America to find a good place where I could live. Dad finally found the perfect place for me: the harbor of New York. In 1884 Dad finally finished me. But there was a problem: I didn't know how to get to the USA – I was definitely too high to travel just like that on a ship. So I was packed into different boxes and shipped to America – I can tell you – that wasn't a nice journey! Just imagine you were put into 300 pieces and 214 boxes and shipped to America
…
When I arrived in the USA my new home wasn't finished so I had to wait another two years before I was finally presented to the American people. But they really gave me a nice welcome and loved me right from the start. Well, I'm still standing in the harbor of New York today and now it's me who gives visitors to New York a warm welcome. You can come and visit me if you want to – my address is Liberty Island, New York, USA."

KV 3 2 Idiomatic English

b) *Lösungsvorschläge:*
You might feel on top of the world if you have got an A in a Maths test.
You can say that someone needs to let off steam when he's had a bad day, e.g. because a teacher or a friend has been really unfair to him, and he needs to do or say something that makes him feel better.
You might have ants in your pants before a big football match or before you have to play a role in a theatre play. You can't sit still and are excitedly running around.
If your best friend has got a new girlfriend and doesn't talk or think of anything else he is head over heels in love.
The girl who got the leading role in the new theatre production might be proud as a peacock.
After eight lessons at school and just a small lunch, you could eat a horse when you come home.

b) *Lösungsvorschlag:*
"Hi Gemma. This is Sam. Something really terrible happened today! It's really awful! There's this boy from my sports club, Wayne. He's really nice. He's also cute, and I've been secretly in love with him for a long time. But I didn't think he even knew who I was. Today I met him on the bus. He was sitting in the back row.
I didn't get a seat but I stood next to him. I said "Hi". He just looked at me and didn't say a word. I felt really stupid. He was just talking to a girl who was sitting next to him. I'd never seen her before. And then something really embarrassing happened. All of a sudden the bus suddenly stopped and I fell onto him! Oh my God! It was really embarrassing and some of the other passengers on the bus started to laugh. My head turned red. And he looked really angry. I said sorry and he just mumbled something, but I didn't understand him.
I just got off at the next stop, but before I left I looked at him one more time. And do you know what he was doing? He was kissing this girl who was sitting next to him. I didn't take a second look, I just left the bus …"

KV 4 A guided bus tour through New York

a) You: Er heißt uns herzlich zur Bustour durch New York willkommen. Er heißt Richard Wood und er ist heute unser Stadtführer. Wir werden an der Brooklyn Bridge beginnen, die New Yorks Stadtteil Brooklyn mit Manhattan auf der anderen Seite der Brücke verbindet. Die Brooklyn Bridge ist eine der ältesten Hängebrücken der USA und wurde 1883 eröffnet.
…
You: How many boroughs does New York have?
…
You: Brooklyn und Manhattan sind zwei von fünf New Yorker Stadtbezirken. Die anderen heißen Queens, die Bronx und Staten Island. Manhattan ist der älteste Stadtbezirk. Wir werden uns jetzt diesen Stadtteil ansehen.
…
You: New York hat eine lange Einwanderungsgeschichte. 36% der 8.000.000 New Yorker wurden außerhalb der Vereinigten Staaten geboren und kommen aus verschiedenen Ländern. Wahrscheinlich haben wir uns schon gedacht, wo die Menschen, die hier wohnen, herkommen. Wir sind in Chinatown. Wir können uns die tollen Häuser ansehen, in einem der Restaurants oder Imbisse chinesisches Essen probieren oder einen buddhistischen Tempel besichtigen. Chinatown ist die größte chinesische Gemeinde außerhalb von China.
…
You: When did the first Chinese immigrants come to the USA?
…
You: Die ersten chinesischen Einwanderer kamen in den 1850er Jahren in die USA, als in Kalifornien Gold gefunden wurde. Die meisten Chinesen kamen aber nach dem zweiten Weltkrieg. Auch heute noch kommen viele Chinesen in die USA.
…
You: Wir sind jetzt in Greenwich Village, das die New Yorker „the Village" nennen. Das ist ein alter Stadtteil und sieht wegen der alten Häuser und wenigen Hochhäuser auch heute noch ein bisschen wie ein Dorf aus. In den 1950er Jahren zogen viele Künstler und Studenten nach Greenwich Village. Heute ist dieses Viertel für die meisten Künstler und Studenten zu teuer und sie sind in andere Viertel gezogen.
…
You: In which part of New York do artists live today?
…
You: Viele Künstler leben in Soho, einem anderen Stadtteil. Dort gibt es auch viele Galerien.
…
You: Jetzt sind wir an der Kreuzung der 5th Avenue und der 34. Straße. Er sagt, dass es einfach ist, sich in New York zurechtzufinden, weil die Stadt wie ein Gitternetz angelegt ist. Hier ist das Empire State Building. Es hat 102 Stockwerke und ist 443 Meter hoch. 1931 wurde es fertiggestellt und war über 40 Jahre lang das höchste Gebäude, bis das World Trade Center in den 1970er Jahren gebaut wurde.
…
You: What is the highest building in New York today?
… .

You: Nach den Anschlägen auf das World Trade Center ist das Empire State Building wieder der höchste Wolkenkratzer in New York. Wenn das One World Trade Center fertiggestellt hat, wird dieses das höchste Gebäude der Stadt sein.

b) *Lösungsvorschlag:*
Now we are at the intersection of Broadway and 42nd street. This is one of the most famous attractions for tourists – Times Square. With all the lights Times Square is even more exciting when it's dark so you need to come back tonight. There are a lot of theaters here and you can come and watch the big Broadway musicals, but there are also a lot of shops, fast food restaurants, cafés and a lot more.

Here we are at Central Park. New Yorkers and tourists love this park right in the center of Manhattan. It's about 2.5 miles long and 0.5 miles wide. There are many lakes and it's just a beautiful and peaceful place in the middle of the city. A lot of New Yorkers come here to relax or to go jogging. It's especially beautiful in spring time.

Unit 2

KV 2 When should British teenagers be allowed to drive?

c) *Lösungsvorschlag:*
"Children should be allowed to leave school when they are 14"
The number of years children have to stay at school has changed a lot over the last hundred years and it's different in different countries. I think it's something which needs to be thought about regularly.
The main point is that if children don't have to go to school, then their parents might decide to make them go to work so that they can earn some money. This has always happened and still happens today in some countries even though it is illegal. When children live with their parents, it's difficult for them to choose the best thing for themselves.
Secondly, even if their parents let them go to school, some children would decide against it even if it was the best thing for them. When children are 14, they don't understand what life is really like, and they shouldn't have to. When they have to go to school, there are people who can help them choose the right things to do.
On the other hand many young people go to school for two or three years and don't learn anything. Also, when they are bored at school, they make it difficult for other pupils to learn, too.
Secondly, the education system could be changed so that young people could take a year or more out of school and work or do some training, but then go back to school if they want to. If people had the choice, they might take their lives and education more seriously.
In summary I believe that the discussion is a lot more complicated than the title says. There are a lot more choices to be made. Children should be able to leave school, but not be allowed to sit around and do nothing. They should also be able to go back to school if they want to.

KV 3 1 Students shouldn't have to do sport at school after they're 16

a) For:
You can drop other subjects, so why not sport?
When you leave school, you don't have to do sport.
You don't have to do sport to stay fit.
Lots of things are good and important, but you can't do everything. There just isn't enough time.

Against:
There are too many people who are overweight.
It's important to be fit in body and mind.
It's been shown that sport helps you to think better, too.

b) *Lösungsvorschlag:*
Partner B: I don't think you should have to do sport at school after you're 16.
Partner A: I'm afraid I don't agree. Sport is really important because it's important to stay healthy.
Partner B: Yes, I can see your point, but there are other ways to stay healthy. I always cycle to school, for example.
Partner A: Well, you're right there, but there are too many people who are overweight and if they did more sport at school, it wouldn't be such a problem.
Partner B: Of course, that's true, but if they left school, they wouldn't have to do sport anyway.
Partner A: That might be true, but I don't think it's a good argument. If students did sport at school, they'd be fitter and healthier and they might learn to enjoy it.
Partner B: Yes, they might learn to enjoy it, but lots of things are good and important and you can't do everything. There's just too little time.

c) *Lösungsvorschlag:*
Partner A: I don't think you should have to do sport at school after you're 16.
Partner B: Yes, but you only think that because you don't like sport.
Partner A: That's not true. I like sport but I don't like the sports at our school. I like …
Partner B: It doesn't matter what you like. The point is that you'd be fitter if you did more sport.
Partner A: I am fit.
Partner B: No, you aren't, and you'd be more intelligent. People who …
Partner A: More intelligent? I'm a lot more intelligent than you! Just because you like football, you think everybody should do football and …
Partner B: Football is a very intelligent game. If more people played ….
Partner A: Football?! Intelligent?! What a joke!

d) *Lösungsvorschlag:*
In the impolite discussion, I didn't listen to my partner as much. I didn't want to know his opinion. I didn't always believe what I said – I just argued so that I could win the argument. But it was more fun.

2 School improvements

a) *Lösungsvorschläge:*
I think we should be allowed to do more sports.
I think we should have longer breaks so that we have more time for sports or talking to our friends.

Unit 3

KV 1 All's well that ends well?

Lösungsvorschlag:
Frances and Gordon, an English couple, had been looking forward to travelling around the American West together for months. They had both saved thousands of dollars so that they could travel together for six months.
The first month had been wonderful too, but when they started to tour the desert of Nevada things had got more difficult. Frances was a bit nervous because she was always worried that a spider would be in her sleeping bag. Gordon was also worried – that they hadn't brought

enough water with them. They started to argue more often and have less fun.
One morning they both woke up and both felt tired. They had breakfast together quite happily but then Gordon drank the rest of the water and Frances went crazy. Gordon hadn't asked her; he'd just drunk it all himself. Frances shouted at him and told him he was selfish. Gordon shouted back. Neither of them could remember later what they said but at some point Frances got so angry she told him that she never wanted to see him again. She got in the car and tried to drive away. Gordon realized that that was stupid – she couldn't drive away on her own with no water. He tried to stop her but she carried on driving. The car hit him and then the gate and then she drove off. Gordon had fallen to the ground but wasn't hurt. He felt terrible – what a stupid argument – but then he saw something on the ground. What was it? Oil?
Frances drove and drove and then saw some smoke. Was it coming out of her engine? Suddenly the car stopped and Frances climbed out of the car. She looked at the engine but there was nothing she could do. Suddenly she realized that she was thirsty and got a bottle from the car. She drank the last bit of it. Oh no! What should she do now? She wouldn't last long without any water. She looked around and saw something in the distance. Was that a small lake? Yes, it was. She was sure. She put something on her head and started to walk.
Back at the camp, when Gordon realized that something was wrong with the car, he ran after it and hoped that she would stop soon, but she didn't. She drove away.
He stopped and turned around. What could he do now? He went back to the campsite and asked the woman in the office what he could do. She called the emergency services and a helicopter came out. An hour later he was in the helicopter looking down at the ground. They could follow the car tracks for some time but then lost them when it got windy and blew sand over them. They flew for hours but couldn't find her. Gordon had almost given up hope when he saw the car and, a little distance away, Frances, below them. They went down and landed next to her. But was she still alive? She was lying down. You can't survive long in the desert with no water.
Two months later, they were back in England. They were still friends and still together. But next time, they said, they'd go to Majorca on holiday.

KV 3 Pocahontas

a) 1. Pocahontas (or Matoaka) was one of the daughters of the Native American chief Powhatan.
2. In 1608 the Native Americans captured one of the colonists, John Smith. Smith was brought to Pocahontas' father Powhatan who wanted him to die.
3. She was called Rebecca Rolfe.
4. In 1607, when Matoaka was probably about eleven or twelve years old, the first white settlers arrived in Chesapeake Bay on the eastern coast of America where Matoaka and her people lived.
5. Pocahontas was taken as a hostage by the English settlers but they treated her well. As a hostage she met John Rolfe, a farmer from England, and fell in love with him. Rolfe and Pocahontas got married in 1614 – it was probably the first marriage between an English colonist and a Native American woman.
6. One year after the birth of their son Thomas in 1616 the Rolfes were invited to come to England.
7. The people in England were fascinated by her because they had never seen a Native American woman before.

b) Name: Rebecca Rolfe, born Matoaka
Born: around 1595
Born in: eastern coast of America
Parents: father: Native American chief Powhatan
Married to: John Rolfe in 1614
Children: one son, Thomas
Died: at the age of 21 in 1617

c) *Lösungsvorschlag:*
Dear sister,
I have arrived with my dear husband John and my son Thomas in a very different world. We travelled by ship and it took us several weeks. For days we didn't see anything but the ocean. But then we finally arrived in this new world. "Welcome home," John said when we arrived in Bristol. I was really confused at first – there were so many people and so many ships and everyone was running around. But John took my hand and we drove in a carriage to a house. It's a real house, a big building made of stone with several rooms, not a tent like we have. It felt really strange – it was so big and I didn't know why they had so many rooms. But in the evening many people came. I didn't know anyone but Thomas knew them. I met his sister and his mother, who are really nice people. A lot more people came to the house that evening (so that's what all the rooms are for) and they were talking and laughing and they ate a lot of food. Everyone wanted to see me and look at me. It was really strange and I was a little bit scared. The English people look very different from us. They all have this white skin and their hair is not only black but has all kinds of colours – gold and red and brown. Then a person came to me and said that he was an artist and that he would like to paint me. I didn't know at first what he wanted but John explained it to me. So I will see him tomorrow. Let's see what he will do.
I hope you are well. I miss you and all the others very much. Everything is so different here – it's cold, it's rainy and it's still very difficult to understand the people. I hope I will see you soon and that we will soon come back to "America" as they call our home.
Love,
Matoaka

KV 4 Looking at ... Polite language

b) *Lösungsvorschläge:*
No, I don't want to go. I'm tired.
→ Oh, I'm sorry but I'm very tired now. I think I'd rather not go (to the party). Do you think you can find someone else?
No, I didn't say that.
→ I'm sorry, I think you misunderstood me.
Get out of my way.
→ Could I just pass? Thank you.
I don't want that one. I want a bigger piece.
→ Oh, I'm sorry. I'm really hungry today. Could I get a bigger piece?
I'm not talking to you. Shut up.
→ Could we talk another time? That'd be great, thanks.
Turn off your phone. It's giving me a headache.
→ I'm sorry, but would you mind turning off your phone? I have a headache.
I don't have any time now. Come back later.
→ I'm sorry. I'm very busy right now. Would you mind coming back later?

c) + d) *Lösungsvorschläge:*
1: Tourist: Excuse me, please?
Man: Yes, can I help you?
Tourist: I was just wondering how old this building might be.
Man: Oh, I don't know. I'm sorry. But I think there's a sign next to the entrance.
Tourist: Oh yes, you're right. I can see it too, now. Thanks. Let's see. "Fairfax House was built in 1762 by John Carr."

Man: Well, I didn't know that. Sounds interesting.
Tourist: Yes, it does. Well, thanks for your help.

2: Tourist: Excuse me, please.
Woman: Hi, do you need help?
Tourist: Oh, yes, thank you. I'm looking for a restroom. Is there a public restroom in the area?
Woman: Let me think … No, I'm sorry. I don't think so. But there's a café over there. The owner is very nice. I'm sure she wouldn't mind if you used her restroom.
Tourist: Oh, thank you very much. I'll ask her. Bye.
Woman: Bye.

3: Tourist: Excuse me, please?
Man: Hello, can I help you?
Tourist: Oh, yes, thank you. That's very kind. I need to get the next bus to Pike Street but I can't find it on the timetable.
Man: Let's see. Pike Street. The 203 and 205 both go to Pike Street.
Tourist: Oh, thank you very much. Can you tell me where they leave from?
Man: Yes, of course. They both leave at the bus station over there, platform 5. The 203 will be there in 5 minutes.
Tourist: Oh, that's great. Thank you very much for your help. Have a nice day.
Man: No problem. Have a nice day.

4: Tourist: Excuse me, please?
Man: Hi, can I help you?
Tourist: Oh, I'm sorry. Uhm, yes. I'm very hungry. Is there a restaurant or a take away somewhere which isn't too expensive?
Man: Oh, I can't think of any restaurant or take away. But wait. There's a nice sandwich shop just around the corner. They've got really good cheese sandwiches.
Tourist: Oh that's sounds great. I just hope I don't miss my bus.
Man: Which bus do you need?
Tourist: I need the 301 to Church Street.
Man: Let's see. The 301 will be here in 20 minutes. You have plenty of time to buy your sandwich.
Tourist: Oh, that's great. Thanks for the information.
Man: No problem. Bye.

KV 5 Mediation: Karl May

a) *Lösungsvorschlag:*
This article is about Karl May, who was a famous German author. He wrote the books about the famous Indian chief Winnetou and his white friend Old Shatterhand. Generations of children have read these books and loved them.
Karl May was born in 1842 in Ernstthal in Saxony. His parents were poor and many of his brothers and sisters died at a young age. He wanted to be a teacher but he got into trouble quite a few times because he stole things. In 1865 he had to go to prison for four years. Later he began to write but he still had money problems. At the age of 50 his so-called travel novels came out which finally made him famous. For the first time in his life Karl May didn't have to care about money. Now his stories were set in the West of the US and told stories about Native Americans and the white people they met. These travel novels also told the stories of the Indian chief Winnetou and his friend Old Shatterhand.
The books were a big success which was surprising especially as Karl May had never been to America. In 1908, 16 years after his travel novels had come out, Karl May finally visited the US for the first time. He used this experience for his last part of the Winnetou story.
Many people loved May's stories, but he himself was probably the one who loved them most. He built a big house and called it "Villa Shatterhand" and in the end he thought that he himself was Old Shatterhand.
He died at the age of 70 in 1912.

b) *Lösungsvorschlag:*
Bestsellerautor: This is an author whose books are sold a lot and who has a lot of success with them.
Sachsen: This is one of the 16 states in Germany. It's in eastern Germany.
Taschenuhr: It's a clock/watch which you can put in your pocket and carry around with you.
Haftstrafe: It's the time you have to spend in prison after you've done something illegal.
Schulden: This is the money you have to borrow from a bank or other people when you don't have any money of your own.
Apachen: It's the name of a Native American tribe which Winnetou belonged to.
Blutsbruder: This is a very close friend. It's called that because people sometimes exchanged drops of their blood as a sign of their friendship.
Realität: This is what the life with real people is called; characters in a book or film aren't real.
Schmied: This is a person whose job it is to make different things out of metal. The metal is put into a fire; it turns really hot so that you can change its form.
Anhängerschaft: This is a large group of fans an author or film star has when he or she has great success.

Unit 4

KV 1 Looking at … Canyonlands National Park

c) *Lösungsvorschlag:*
Der Canyonlands Nationalpark ist einer der weniger bekannten Nationalparks der USA und hat weniger Besucher als beispielsweise der Yellowstone Park, jedes Jahr ungefähr 440.000. Der Park ist erst im Jahr 1964 entstanden und damit eher neu. Das Wetter dort ist warm und trocken und es gibt nur wenige feste Straßen, weil sich der Park in einem wenig besuchten Teil der USA befindet. Es gibt aber einige Besucherzentren.
Man kann im Park viele verschiedene Dinge tun, z.B. wandern, campen, klettern, reiten oder Kanu fahren. Dabei gibt es Flüsse, die für Anfänger geeignet sind und auch solche, die nur etwas für Kanu-Experten sind. Dann gibt es noch den Horseshoe Canyon. Dort gibt es Gemälde, die über 3.000 oder 4.000 Jahre alt sind. Einige der Gemälde sind die ältesten, die je in den USA entdeckt wurden.

KV 2 1 Gerund or infinitive

infinitive	gerund	both forms
to want	to enjoy	to like
to decide	to imagine	to stop
	to look forward to	to begin
	to dream of	to hate
	to dislike	to love
		to forget
		to remember
		to try

KV 4 3 Word families

Lösungsvorschlag:
end: endless, ending
camp: campsite
care: careful, careless, caretaker
help: helpful, unhelpful, helpless
usual: unusual, usually, unusually
fear: fearful, fearless
back: background, backpack, backpacking
beauty: beautiful

Unit 5

KV 2 Different people, different language

a) *Lösungsvorschlag:*
casual: your mother, your father, your best friend, a student from school, your brother, your sister, an old friend from primary school
polite: your English teacher, your grandmother, a young shop assistant in a music shop, a girl/boy you like very much, your aunt, your uncle, your neighbour, a good friend of your parents
very polite: an old shop assistant in a shoe shop, a police officer, the waiter in a restaurant, the mother of a friend, an old woman you don't know

c) *Lösungsvorschlag:*
(your uncle + clothes store)
Rob: Hi Lisa, nice to see you. What are you doing here?
You: Oh, hi Uncle Rob. Nice to see you, too. I'm waiting for a friend.
Rob: What are you two up to? Are you going shopping?
You: Yes, we are. Emma needs a new top and I want to buy a new CD.
Rob: That sounds like a great plan. Well, enjoy your shopping tour and have a nice day.
You: Thanks, Uncle Rob. You too.

KV 3 2 Be the author – write the story

b) *Lösungsvorschlag:*
It was a dark night in Chicago. It had been raining all day and a heavy fog lay over the city. Detective Wallace had come home from another long day. It had been a day full of crime. He was getting tired of his job. "Only two years left," he told himself. "Then I'll be rid of that job and can finally start a quiet life."
The phone rang. Who could it be at that time of night? He answered it. "Yes?" It was Sergeant Ellis, who had been working with him for a year now. He was young and didn't have a lot of experience, but he was a good guy. "Detective Wallace, it's Ellis. We have a problem. We've found a dead body near the Chicago River and we really need you here." Wallace nodded. "I'll be right there. Where are you?" …
When Wallace arrived at the crime scene, there were a lot of police officers there. He saw Ellis, who was standing next to a dead body, and went to talk to him. "What's happened here?" he asked. "He's been shot. The body was found two hours ago by some guys who were going home from a bar." Wallace looked at the dead man who was lying on the ground. He was still young and he was quite handsome. "Do we know who he was?" "Yes, we do. He had his driver's licence with him. His name is Rick Hanson. We also found his cell phone and checked his last calls. The last person he called was Amanda Brooke. We called her and asked her to come here. She's talking to some officers at the moment. Right over there …" Wallace went over to Mrs. Brooke. She was about 60 years old and she looked very angry. "Mrs. Brooke, I'm Detective Wallace. I'd like to talk to you for a minute." "I really don't know what you want from me! I haven't done anything and I want to go home now!" "Mrs. Brooke, you're the last person Mr. Hanson called before he was shot. What did he want from you?" "I've never seen that man in my life. He must have had the wrong number. I don't know …" At that moment, Sergeant Ellis came to them and whispered something in Wallace's ear. "Some police officers have searched her house and found this." He gave Wallace a piece of paper and he read it. "Mrs. Brooke. This is a letter from Mr. Hanson. It says he'll tell your husband everything about your relationship if you don't give him $50,000. Are you still telling me you've never seen him before? I think we'd better continue our conversation at the police station …"

KV 4 The Hollywood Sign

a) 1923: The Hollywood Sign is put up by a real estate company.
1920s and 1930s: The American film industry becomes more and more famous.
1940s: The Hollywood sign looks terrible and the "H" is missing.
1949: The film industry and the City of Los Angeles decide to keep the sign and repair it; now it says "HOLLYWOOD".
1978: The rock musician Alice Cooper decides it's time for a new sign; famous people and companies raise money to build a new sign out of steel.
2005: The sign is freshly painted.

b) *Lösungsvorschlag:*
Simpson: As you all know, we've met here today to talk about the future of the Hollywood Sign. Some real estate companies want to sell the land, take the sign down and build new houses there. Ms. Wright, you work for a real estate company. Do you want to give us your reasons?
Wright: Yes, thank you, Mr. Simpson. My company is of the opinion that the land the Hollywood Sign is built on could be used in a better way. The area is very expensive and if we took the sign down and built new houses, a lot of money could be made.
Daniels: But there are more important things than money! The sign is an important symbol of the film industry and we can't just take it down. It's what L.A. is known for around the world.
Wright: But think of all the new houses that could be built there and the families that could live in them.
Simpson: Ms. Wright, I see what you mean, but I think Ms. Daniels is right. The sign has become a symbol of the film industry and every year many tourists come to see it.
Hoover: Of course you like all the tourists because they bring money into the city. But think about the families who live in the neighbourhood. There are always crowds of tourists and we don't have a quiet minute. I agree with Ms. Wright: The sign should be taken down and new houses should be built where nice families can live.
Daniels: They can always live somewhere else.
Simpson: In my opinion we can't take it down. It should be sold to the city and the sign should be kept forever. The real estate companies and the city of Los Angeles will have to talk about this. Thank you all for your opinions.